S0-AHC-354

The

Most Gruesome

Hauntings

Of

The Midwest

By: Chad Lewis

© 2012 On The Road Publications

All rights reserved. No part of this publication may be reproduced or transmitted in any form or by any means, electrical or mechanical, including photocopy, recording, or any information storage or retrieval system, without the permission in writing from the publisher.

ISBN: 978–0-9824314–5-0

Proudly printed in the United States by Documation

On The Road Publications

3204 Venus Ave

Eau Claire, WI 54703

www.chadlewisresearch.com

chadlewis44@hotmail.com

Cover Design: Kevin Lee Nelson

Dedication

This book is dedicated to the memory of all the victims whose stories are featured. Whether they met death by their own hand, a murder's hand, or simply by the hand of fate, may their spirits find peace.

Contents

Preface

Report Your Experiences- This guide is set up for you to have an adventure. I recommend that all legend trippers bring along at least a camera and journal to document your findings.

Private Property- Unfortunately a couple of the locations listed in this book are on private property. Please respect the privacy of the owners and only view these places from the road. If you do venture onto private property please make sure that you have prior permission, otherwise you may end up with a hefty trespassing ticket to go along with your paranormal sighting.

Safety- Many of these cases come with a side dish of danger. Keep in mind that many of these locations are out in the middle of nowhere, so always try to have someone with you in case of injuries and emergencies.

Accuracy- I have made every effort to ensure this guide is current and accurate yet some errors will inevitably surface. If you find better directions, take better photos, or manage to capture some convincing evidence please contact me so I can make the changes for future editions of this book.

Roadside Attractions- This guide is just the tip of the iceberg of your adventure. Getting to these locations is half the fun, and the U.S. is filled with so many oddities that you should never run out of places to explore. Allot some time to hit all of the odd roadside attractions that you will bump into along your adventure.

Outside the Norm- Veteran legend trippers know that the best adventures come by getting out of your daily routine. Travel the back roads, spend the night at the dodgy roadside motel, and grab a meal at the old mom and pop diner. Trust me the chain businesses will not miss you.

Acknowledgements

I would like to pay my respects to all of the people mentioned in this book who met death in such a horrible manner. I hope that their spirits can someday rest peacefully.

I have to give a big thank you to the many paranormal researchers, folklorists, investigators, and legend trippers that accompanied me on many of these cases including; Terry Fisk, Linda Godfrey, Todd Roll, Michael Coffield, Dawnette Cook and Tamara Gleason.

Once again, bad ass legend trippers Noah Voss and Kevin Nelson were involved in the mayhem of investigating these places. I always find it a suitable challenge to try and keep up with them.

Finally, when you spend endless days and nights immersed in topics of murder, suicide, grave-digging, decapitation, deadly accidents, and human cannibalism, it becomes a struggle to not let the darkness of the cases seep into you. Luckily for me, I had Nisa and Leo to continually keep me grounded in the beauty of life.

Foreword

Chad's adventurous travels through the sometimes blood soaked country side have revealed to his readers for years that truth is indeed at times more disturbing than fiction. Follow along with him on the most gruesome, often gory, and always at least slightly disturbing—to even the most balanced mind.

I've accompanied Chad on a few travels through daring and dangerous locations. Enjoying the journey as much as the destination doesn't preclude him from being an experienced investigative journalist. He's not just looking for the next thrill that naturally comes with visiting these haunting locations. Chad actively searches for clues that illuminate a broader understanding to folklore throughout the Midwest and indeed the world. Chad is from the pre-Internet generation that was forced to find answers by physical visits to county courthouse file rooms, countless phone calls, thumbing through plat records looking for names to connect lore and locations, and purchasing birth and death certificates to verify what had become obscure urban legend. The sometimes lost art of leaving the Internet behind and connecting with actual people, face to face—is not lost on Chad. Tracking down the people who touched the original legend is always telling. Allow Chad to share his story so that you might become completely immersed in *The Most Gruesome Hauntings of the Midwest!*

Ominous warnings of deathly peril from stone faced first hand experiencers of the grotesque, gory, and gruesome were not enough to even delay Chad from trudging forward. He moves. Constantly seeking a story, looking for lore, and always trying to experience firsthand what those brave enough to tell their story have shared.

With this book in hand, will you be the next to report an experience?

-Noah Voss

Founder GetGhostGear.com Enterprises and Author

Mysterious Madison—Unsolved Crimes, Strange Creatures & Bizarre Happenstance

UFO Wisconsin—A Progress Report

Introduction

As much as we hate to admit it, we often find ourselves inexplicably drawn to stories of the macabre. Stories that by all means should repel and sicken us tend to pique our morbid fascination with gruesome events that occur all around us. Many of these tragic events are so horrific that they cast a permanent cloud of darkness over the areas where they occur. When it comes to hauntings, a pattern of cases involving suicide, murder, untimely deaths, bizarre accidents, and serial killings often appears. Is there something so powerful about the manner of these deaths that force those involved to remain among the living as ghosts and spirits? The best way for you to answer that question is by visiting these places for yourselves. But I must warn you, the haunted cases featured in this book are all gruesome. Not gruesome in some detached Hollywood torture movie way, but gruesome in a psychological way, a way that slowly seeps into your mind and refuses to exit.

This is a collection of the most horrifying cases that I have ever investigated. I have been working on some of these cases for nearly two decades, while others have only caught my attention over the last few years. Having traveled around the world to the creepiest places on earth I felt I was well accustomed to stories of death and horrific human behavior. But I must confess that the act of putting all of these horrible cases into one book took its toll. My dreams were terrorized by these gruesome cases. Bloody reenactments of young Julie Markham chopping her seven kids to pieces and Ed Gein wearing the decomposing skin of his desecrated victims danced through my nightly dreams.

Many of these places have been forever cursed by the dreadful events that have transpired, making it nearly impossible for even the most seasoned legend tripper not to shudder a bit while visiting them. Even if you are like me and possess no psychic ability, you cannot help getting the chills while walking through a room where an entire family was slaughtered or be overcome with the sense that something is not quite right at the rural cemetery where the dead are said to walk. I took comfort and solace in knowing that even after immersing myself for years in all these gory cases, they still had not lost their impact on me.

Keep an eye out,

Chad Lewis

Bloody Bride Bridge

Location:

Highway 66—Crossing the Plover River
Stevens Point, WI

Haunting:

The majority of people passing over the Plover River along Highway 66 have no idea of the gory event that transpired along their route. While the bridge's general appearance does nothing to distinguish it from every other run-of-the-mill bridge, its grisly history certainly gives it a sorted past. Steeped in legend, the bridge is known to many locals as "Bloody Bride Bridge." The general legend of the bridge goes something like this. Many years ago, a newlywed couple was returning home on the night of their wedding celebration. The ceremony had gone off without a hitch, and the gushing bride felt like the luckiest woman on earth. Having no idea that their luck was about to take a terrible turn for the worse, the couple was involved in a horrendous car accident as they passed over the bridge. Still dressed in her beautiful wedding gown, which was now covered in her blood, the bride could only pray that help would soon arrive. Unfortunately, her injuries were too severe, and her marital bliss was dramatically cut short as she bled to death waiting for assistance that arrived too late.

Not long after her untimely death, passersby began spotting the ghost of the young bride staggering along the bridge where she met her fate. One of the first appearances of the bloody bride was said to have come when a police officer was crossing over the bridge. Out of nowhere, a young woman in a bloody dress suddenly appeared in the middle of the road. Unable to stop in time, the officer slammed on the brakes as his screeching car smashed into the woman. After coming to a jarring stop, the officer reluctantly turned back to see the damage, fearing that the woman's mangled body would be scattered all across the pavement. Much to his amazement, not only was the woman not strewn across the road, she was actually sitting in his back seat, covered in blood. Over the years, the telling and re-telling of the police officer's tale spawned the dare of Bloody Bride Bridge. The dare states that if you go to the area late at night, park your vehicle on the side of the bridge and look into the rear view mirror, the ghost of the bloodied bride will appear in your backseat.

The Bloody Bridge is along Highway 66

The Most Gruesome Hauntings of the Midwest

In 2008, I received a report from a woman who described herself as an "intuitive healer" who was able to "sense ghosts and energy" ever since she was a small child. Having heard the story of the haunting, the woman and her friend headed to the bridge in hopes of being able to pick up on the energy of the bloody bride. Once at the bridge, the woman wandered off to a nearby bench and sat down to concentrate on the spirit. Suddenly, she began to "feel energy" start to form both around her and directly next to her. Convinced that the spirit of an unknown woman was now sitting right beside her on the bench, the intuitive began trying to communicate with the spirit. Unfortunately, the spirit departed before the intuitive could gather any relevant information to determine if the visiting ghost was the bloody bride.

Over the years, I have received roughly half a dozen reports from those who claim that while passing over the bridge they saw the apparition of a woman wearing a wedding dress caked with blood. I, myself, have spent over a dozen nights parked on the bridge waiting for the ghost to appear, only to leave empty-handed (or in this case, empty-seated). Since I first heard of this case back in the early 2000s, I have been trying to determine the real history and to sort fact from fiction. In 2002, I visited the Stevens Point police station hoping to find a report detailing the deadly accident. One would think that if such a terrible accident did in fact take place at the bridge, it might be something that stuck in people's memory. At the police station, I recapped the legend for several officers, all of whom had no recollection of any accident or death occurring around the Highway 66 bridge. However, I did discover that if the bride did die on the bridge, it would have been investigated by the sheriff's department, not the police department. So off I went to the sheriff's department where I talked with several deputies, each having more years of experience than the last, only to find out that—much like the police department—no one had heard of a woman dying out on the bridge.

Those who park on the bridge often encounter the bloody bride

With little concrete evidence regarding the accident and/or death of the young bride, it begs the question of whether this case is anything more than an urban legend. Before you write this case off, though, remember that there are several possible reasons why no record or memory of the accident has surfaced. Keep in mind that we know very little about the date in which the accident was said to have occurred. Outside of knowing that it involved an automobile, and not a horse and buggy, we haven't even narrowed it down to a specific decade. It is possible that the accident happened so long ago that the original report was lost, burned, thrown away, or destroyed long ago. Back in the non-digital record keeping system, non-murder cases—or those of similar importance—were rarely kept on file for longer than seven years. An accident occurring fifty or sixty years ago would also explain the lack of memory from those I interviewed. Of course, we also have to consider that the reason no historical evidence or corroboration has surfaced is due to the fact that the accident never truly happened, and the story is nothing more than an urban legend. But, even if we still do not have a smoking gun proving the existence of the bloody bride, you may want to keep an eye out while on the bridge—just in case!

The Lost Village of Pere Cheney

Location:

Now a secluded cemetery
Beaver Creek Township, MI

Haunting:

You won't find the village of Pere Cheney on any modern maps, and if you rely solely on your GPS to take you there, you will be out of luck as well. For all intents and purposes, the town of Pere Cheney no longer exists. It is hard to imagine that a once bustling lumber town that enjoyed a hotel, Western Union, school, depot, several sawmills, and the C.S. Hutt general store would now be nothing more than a fading memory. Maybe I am being a bit dramatic here, because even though all the stores, homes, and people have long since faded from the area, a few remnants of the town still exist— including the old cemetery and the numerous wandering spirits that haunt it.

This case provides an interesting contradiction. Normally when a town has been gone for nearly a century, people tend to forgot that it even existed. Yet, when I traveled to the area to investigate this case, I discovered that the town of Pere Cheney was well known with nearly everyone I spoke with. At first glance, this doesn't seem to make any sort of sense, but when you factor in the legend that the area is cursed with death and heartache, the fascination of keeping Pere Cheney alive becomes crystal clear. The main legend told to me by person after person went like this. In the early days of the state, the town of Pere Cheney seemed destine to prosper. The town was chalk full of people and commerce alike. But as fate would have it, prosperity was not in the cards for the new town, and in during the 1880s the village was ravaged by diphtheria. In order to stop the spread of the infectious disease and spare additional families from death, the town took the drastic measure of burning down what remained of the town. Being the hearty folk that they were, the town was soon rebuilt and residents began to carry on with their everyday lives. Just as things were returning to normal, a second deadly wave of disease ripped through the village, wiping out scores of people. Superstitious folks began worrying that perhaps the town was cursed and that people ought to leave the town while they still could. By the early 1900s, the town was completely abandoned, inhabited only by the souls of those who met their end in Pere Cheney.

Nearly Abandoned Pere Cheney Graveyard

The Most Gruesome Hauntings of the Midwest

The combination of death, disease, and cursed land come together to make a wonderfully intriguing and gruesome story, but is the tantalizing legend accurate? After digging through the old newspaper accounts, talking with the local historical society, and speaking with local residents, I have pieced together how the story really unfolded . . . and unfortunately it still remains just as dark and tragic as the legend says. In 1883, the town was ravaged by a bout of diphtheria that took the lives of many local children. Diphtheria is an acute infectious disease spread mainly by coughing, sneezing, or by contaminated objects or foods. By all accounts it is a gruesome disease where a thick sheet of gray/black material starts to build on your throat, pushes against your windpipe, and forces you to struggle for air. In the 1800s, deadly illnesses were part of the daily lives of people who amazingly rebounded very quickly from great loss and were not easily displaced from their land. Ten years later, in 1893, the town was once again struck with smallpox, scarlet fever, and diphtheria, resulting in another large round of deaths, many of which can be verified by the cemetery gravestones. Believe it or not, in 1906, diphtheria once again punished the town with death and misery. With three major outbreaks in such a limited span of time, it is easy to see why people might have considered the town to be cursed. By 1914, the town of Pere Cheney was all but abandoned. However, I was unable to find any evidence that the town was burned down in protest to fate. It seems much more plausible that residents simply got siphoned away in search of economic opportunities to the larger cities of Grayling and Roscommon.

No one is quite sure as to the origin of the cemetery's haunted reputation. Many seniors of the area that I spoke with recalled hearing stories of the place being haunted while they were youngsters. For decades the cemetery was left desecrated and in a state of continual disrepair. Weeds and tall grass had overtaken the once manicured grounds, vandals had ruthlessly busted up and kicked over gravestones, and trash was strewn about the place like it was a county dump. Luckily, in 1989, the Grayling branch of the VFW started the process of returning the cemetery to its once pristine condition. Graves were put back together, the unruly field was cut, and a flag pole was erected. All the attention placed on the cemetery was also thought to be the driving force in resurrecting the haunted stories. The total seclusion of the cemetery tends to attract many teenagers who go there to party away from the watchful eye of their parents or the police. I spoke with a group of friends that had driven out to the cemetery to party and camp the night away. It was a long night and numerous beers had been consumed and discarded throughout the cemetery, when the group finally drifted off to sleep. When the blazing sun finally awoke the sleeping teens, they noticed that all the beer cans had been picked up and thrown neatly into the garbage can. They believed that the spirits had cleaned up the cemetery while they slept.

There are many unmarked graves throughout this rural cemetery

Teenagers are not the only ones drawn to the cemetery, as I spoke with a local man in his 40s who would often walk out to the cemetery to check out the all of the old grave markers. He said that every time he walked through the cemetery he would get the odd sense that he was not alone; he felt as though some unseen presence was watching his every move. On several occasions, these odd feelings would occur just before he saw several strange figures moving throughout the cemetery. The man never did find out who or what the figures were. One of the most popular legends of the cemetery involves a woman that lived in Pere Cheney. Apparently townsfolk believed that the woman was a witch, so they dragged her from town out to the cemetery where she was hanged and burned on a tree, forever trapping her spirit to the cemetery. Although I found no actual accounts of any 'witch' or non-witch being hanged and burned in the cemetery, I did coincidently, speak with several witnesses who told similar stories of seeing the ghostly image of a woman hanging from one of the cemetery trees.

Be warned though, this cemetery is exceptionally hard to get to. Even with detailed directions, I found myself turned around more times than I cared to count. After several hours of frustrated maneuvering, I finally found an access point leading to the cemetery, yet the lone road was so gutted with treacherous groves and deep potholes, it became impassable. Exiting the car, I had no choice but to walk the final portion of roadway. With my first step into the cemetery, I could immediately see why the place had taken on such a haunted reputation. With broken and scattered gravestones, overgrown vegetation, and an overall uneasy feeling to it, the cemetery looked like something straight out of a horror movie. After reading over many of the diphtheria victims' gravestones, it became quite clear this horror movie was all too real. Knowing that many of those buried in the cemetery met a horrible end only enhanced the sadness that seemed to seep directly from the gravesites. I once saw a play where the premise was that you remained in Heaven only as long as there was someone living that remembered you. As I strolled through the grounds I couldn't help but wonder if the spirits haunting this old cemetery were merely trying to keep the memory of Pere Cheney alive just a little bit longer.

Tragedy at the Heritage House

Location:

4789 Salo Road
Embarrass, MN

Haunting:

When it comes to belief in the paranormal, many people subscribe to the old adage that seeing is believing. Yet for others, it may be that believing equals seeing. Let me explain. Talking with thousands of witnesses over the past 20 years, I have come to the conclusion that if someone goes into a visit to a haunted location with the belief that they are going to have a paranormal experience, it is much more likely that they will have a paranormal experience. Hence, believing equals seeing. The strange case of the haunted Heritage House is a prime example of this theory.

Those who park on the bridge often encounter the ghost of the drowned boy

The small, tightly knit town of Embarrass, Minnesota takes exceptional pride in its sizeable Finnish heritage. Each summer the town proudly provides tours of surviving Finnish homes, buildings, and various other farm structures that still remain throughout the area. Of course, when you have such a long and rich history, there are bound to be some legends attached to it as well. For decades the town had found itself smack dab in the middle of one of Northern Minnesota's most infamous legends—the haunting of the old Pyhala farmstead. You can find the Heritage House legend on countless websites, numerous books, and several short amateur documentaries. Each of these sources basically tell the same story of the Pyhala family, pioneers who emigrated from Finland to brave the wildlands of Minnesota's Northwoods. The legend states that during an especially harsh and brutal winter the family could do nothing but bunker down inside their home as they tried to survive season's relentless brutality. The lack of sunlight, coupled with the tight quarters of such a large family was too much for the father to handle, propelling him into a complete psychotic breakdown. When spring finally arrived he took his young son William down to the Embarrass River, where he told him that Jesus was able to walk on water and so should he. With that, he forced young William into the deep dark churning waters, where he met his watery grave in the freezing river. Now the dare is that if anyone is brave enough to park their car on the small bridge above the Embarrass River they will encounter the spirit of the drowned boy. He will act much like a siren and beckon you out with cries of help that are meant to try to lure you into the water, where he will attempt to pull you under.

Riverbank where young Billy Pyhala met his fate

The beauty of this legend is that it takes several aspects of truth and blends it with a dash of pure fiction to create the perfect haunted tale. I am always amazed by how just many paranormal "research" groups fail to do anything outside of consulting Google or Wikipedia during their investigations. Before we get to all of the paranormal activity that happens in the area, let's start at the beginning with the true history of the story. In 1902, the Pyhala family immigrated to the US from Finland and settled down in the Northern Minnesota. In 1909, Mikko and his wife Anna purchased land in Embarrass for their family home. Tragedy struck in 1916, when young Isaac William (Billy) Pyhala did, in fact, drown in the Embarrass River. However, unlike the tantalizing legend, Mikko played no part in the unfortunate drowning of his son. In his book, *God Led My Steps*, Verner Pyhala (Billy's brother) told of the family story surrounding Billy's death. One September morning, Billy talked two of his brothers into constructing a raft that they could use to cross over the Embarrass River which served as the family's favorite fishing and swimming hole. Brave Billy guided his raft onto the river, while his brothers excitedly watched from the shore. In a matter of minutes Billy was suddenly sucked under by the strong current. When Billy did not re-appear his brother ran off to alert their father, who grabbed a large pole as he rushed to the river to help save his son. Neighbors heard the commotion and rushed to the riverbanks to help find young Billy. According to Verner, "After what seemed like hours, they finally found Billy's body, and pulled him out to the bank of the river. Those who had some CPR experience worked on Billy for almost an hour trying to bring him back to life. They finally pronounced him dead." When I got a copy of Billy's death certificate I discovered that he had not died in the spring as the erroneous legend claims, but instead the death certificate states that six-year-old Billy died on September 12, 1912. The death certificate also listed Billy's cause of death as being "accidental drowning" which adds even more proof that Billy's father played no part in his son's death. Contrary to the legend, Verner wrote that "it was the saddest day in my father's life. My father told me about this tragedy many times during my growing up."

Billy's death certificate lists the cause of death as Accidental Drowning

Even though most people had the details of Billy's drowning slightly mixed up, the fact remains that Billy did indeed drown in the Embarrass River. A small bridge does pass over the area of the drowning, and this is where most of the activity is said to take place. Each year I hear several stories from legend trippers who claim that as soon as they parked their car on the bridge they could see and hear the ghostly apparition of a young boy in the water below. Others claim to hear unexplained heavy splashing coming from the river, as though someone is swimming even though no swimmer is ever found. Other out of place noises can also be heard while walking down near the river. During my years of research into the case I have parked on the bridge over a dozen times as I eagerly waited for the apparition of young Billy to appear. Unfortunately (or maybe fortunately) for me, each time I have visited, young Billy has not made his presence known.

Over the years vandals have trashed the inside of the home

In addition to the bridge, odd happening are also said to occur inside the old Pyhala home (Heritage House). At one time the only stories I heard about were from the bridge, but more recently I have noticed that the legends have morphed and progressed to the point that they now include the old house. Those who visit the house (illegally) claim that if you walk up to the second floor of the building you will be chased out by the angry ghost of Mr. Pyhala. One of most regrettable aspects of this case is that, in a never-ending quest to experience the paranormal, hordes of young legend trippers break in to the historic home only to leave it trashed and vandalized. My recommendation is that you enjoy the legend from the legally safe bridge over the Embarrass River. However, if you really want a chance to experience the history and lore of the Heritage House you can sign up for one of the official Heritage Homestead Tours given throughout the summer where you can see the Finish history and support the upkeep of the buildings at the same time. Just don't expect to hear any ghost stories on your tour, as the town is quick to point out that it is their belief that the home and entire area are not haunted by any ghosts. Have fun on your adventure and remember that sometimes seeing is believing.

The Crash of Flight 232

Sioux City, Iowa

The Crash of Flight 232

Location:

Sioux City Airport
2403 Ogden Ave.
Sioux City, Iowa 51111
www.flysiouxgateway.com

Haunting:

Symptoms of Pteromerhanophobia (the fear of flying) include hyperventilation, heart palpitations, vomiting, shaking, nausea, dizziness, and even panic attacks. If you suffer from the fear of flying, you may want to do yourself a favor and skip over this case. This is one of those good news/bad news scenarios. The bad news is that on July 19, 1989, United Flight 232 took off from Stapleton International Airport in Colorado bound to Philadelphia International Airport in Pennsylvania with 285 passengers when it underwent an engine failure of its number two engine. Unable to maneuver, the pilot lost control and the plane crashed into the Sioux City Airport, killing 110 passengers and 11 crew members. The good news is that not all of those on board Flight 232 died in the crash. Among the survivors were 175 passengers and 10 crew members. The number of fatalities would have been much higher if not for the extremely well trained rescue crews that were credited with saving many lives. Captain Haynes believed there were three reasons why so many people survived the crash. First, the crash occurred during the daylight hours, making the response much easier. Secondly, the crash took place during a shift change at the regional trauma center and the burn center, providing twice the number of personnel on hand to help the survivors. And lastly, the Iowa National Guard was on duty at the airport. The official cause of the crash was originally blamed on poor maintenance by the airline, yet follow up investigations believed the crash was caused by a faulty part. The plane crash was the subject of a TV movie. In 1992, the movie "Crash Landing: The Rescue of Flight 232" aired. The crash was also featured on the National Geographic Channel's "Seconds From Disaster" show.

Unidentified screams can be heard coming from the airport

The relatively small regional airport has seen its fair share of paranormal activity. Flyers often arrive at the airport only to be greeted by the strange sounds of people screaming in pain. Since no source of the mysterious screaming can be located, it is usually just brushed off by the witnesses, most of whom are unaware of the tragedy of Flight 232. Inside the airport, mysterious moans can also be heard as flyers dart by to catch their planes. The most compelling events involve the actual sighting of nearly transparent figures moving through the airport before disappearing into the walls. Those who have seen these wandering spirits believe they are the victims of Flight 232.

The sound of mysterious crying often travel through the airport

Unfortunately, I have not had the privilege of flying from the Sioux City Airport. When I investigated this case I decided to take the more dangerous route of arriving by car. In a case where over 150 people died, it gets very hard to narrow down a ghost to just one or two people. With this case, the spirit(s) haunting the airport could have been anyone who died in the crash, an aviation enthusiast, or someone altogether unknown. When my inquires into the crash were met with blank stares, I assumed that either the workers had not heard of Flight 232 or that they just weren't too keen on talking about plane crashes while inside an airport. In fact, while traveling, most of us tend to block out the thought of our plane crashing. The victims of Flight 232 have no such luxury . . . which is maybe why their spirits continue to haunt the very spot where their life came to a screeching halt.

St. Valentine's Day Massacre

Location:

2122 North Clark Street
Chicago, Illinois

Haunting:

In 1929, Prohibition gangster Al Capone had his hand firmly entwined in every illegal activity that Chicago could offer. Capone was looking to expand his criminal reign and that meant the annihilation of rival gang leader George "Bugs" Moran. To accomplish this mission, Capone hatched a detailed plan that was initiated by his traveling down to Florida where he would establish an air-tight alibi for what was about to go down. Tucked away in the Sunshine State, Capone made sure he was highly visible to the public while several of his colleagues put the final touches on their deadly plan. On the morning of February 14, the Moran gang met at a North Clark

Street garage under the false assumption that they were about to receive a large shipment of some treasured Canadian liquor. Instead, what they were about to receive was an unfriendly visit from some deadly gangsters. Capone's plan called for a bit of subterfuge, as several of his men dressed themselves as Chicago police officers and arrived at Moran's garage in a two large cars. In was approximately 10:30 am when Moran, who was running late for the meeting, saw the "police" arrive and thought it was a bust, so he hightailed it out of the area. It was a fortunate move on Moran's part because Capone's men busted into the garage and demanded that the seven gangsters gathered inside drop their weapons and get up against the wall. Thinking that this was just a traditional bust with the police shaking them down for a cut of the profits, Moran's men complied with the order. By the time they realized the men were not police officers, it was too late. *The Appleton Post Crescent* wrote that the gangsters "herded their helpless and unarmed victims to the rear and mercilessly executed them with a wave of shotguns and machine guns, every body bearing from six to ten bullets." The lone survivor of the massacre was the garage dog; it was barking so loudly it attracted the attention of the neighbor lady, who instructed one of her tenants to go over and find out what all the barking was about. Once inside, the gentleman discovered the bloody mess and quickly notified the authorities.

The original massacre building is no longer there

By the time the real police arrived at the scene, all seven of the men were dead or in the process of dying. According to the *Woodland Daily Democrat,* "Several of the victims appeared to have attempted to run after being shot but none of them got far. The bodies were in all parts of the room. One body remained unidentified because of the top of the head had been blown off." The dog was in such an agitated state that it became impossible to quiet and eventually had to be put down. The media dubbed the killing as the "St. Valentine's Day Massacre" and, although no one was ever convicted of the murders, it was widely thought that the killings had Capone's fingerprints all over them. When reporters asked Moran—who luckily escaped fate that day—who he thought was responsible for the crime, he allegedly stated that "only Capone kills like that."

This massacre served as a turning point in the public's perception of the brutal gang wars. This barbaric act had finally pushed the public to call out for a real crackdown on underworld characters. When the gun smoke finally settled on the St. Valentine's Day Massacre, Capone may have opened himself up to more than just increased scrutiny and hostility from the city... he may have add some ghostly spirits as well. From the time of the St. Valentine's Day Massacre forward, he was convinced that a spirit from of one of the seven gun-downed gangsters was continually haunting him. Capone carried this belief with him until the day he died.

The gruesome aftereffects of the brutal gangland massacre

The former massacre site sits along the heavily used North Clark Street. Each day hordes of unsuspecting pedestrians pass by the massacre site, totally oblivious to the area's deadly past. Unfortunately in 1967, the City of Chicago tore down the old garage in an attempt to rid itself of any gangster history. Today, the old garage site is nothing more than an unassuming grassy front yard. But those who know their history report that even though the massacre building is gone, the crime has not been forgotten. While walking down the sidewalk, pedestrians will hear the sound of rapid gunshots blasting off. Being that it is Chicago, most people are used to hearing gunfire . . . yet the sudden, almost machine gun-like nature of the mysterious gunfire leads many researchers to believe that the witnesses are actually hearing the phantom firing from the old Tommy Guns. The sporadic appearance of seven shadowy figures roaming the site lends credence to the idea that the fallen gangsters are forever trapped to the location.

Even more bizarre is the idea that perhaps humans are not the only species to pick up on the paranormal aura of the massacre site. Those who routinely walk their dogs past the massacre site notice that their pets often exhibit unusual behavior. Many dogs will suddenly turn fearful and begin to whine and cower as they quickly try to pass by. Other dogs will have the exact opposite reaction, and the owners will find themselves in possession of excitedly loud and aggressive dogs that seems to be barking and snapping at some unseen presence. Is it possible that our canine friends are picking up on some sort of paranormal activity that remains hidden to us humans? Based on how out of character their dogs act at the site, many passersby would say yes.

While Capone's name will forever be tied to the St. Valentine's Day Massacre, it appears that his spirit will not. That honor falls on Mount Carmel Cemetery in Hillside, Illinois, where the spirit of Capone is frequently spotted walking the site of his family burial plot.

The Ill-fated Love Affair At Forepaugh's Restaurant

Location:

Forepaugh's Restaurant
276 Exchange Street S
St. Paul, MN 55102
(612) 224–5606

Haunting:

In Hollywood, no matter how unbelievable and convoluted the romance becomes, nearly every love story ends with an uplifting, happy ending. Yet in the real world, many love stories come crashing down in tragedy…

like that of Joseph Forepaugh. By all outside appearances, in the late 1800s Forepaugh seemed to have everything a man could wish for. He operated a very respected and profitable business. He lived in a Victorian mansion that was situated in one of the most exclusive areas in the entire Twin Cities, and he had the love of his healthy and growing family. But all the success wasn't enough for Forepaugh, as legend states that he began a fiery affair with one of his hired housekeepers, a woman named Molly. It didn't take long for their intimate secret to get discovered—as soon as Forepaugh's wife heard of the torrid affair, she forbade him from every seeing Molly again. This decision sent him on a spiral of depression from which the consequences would be devastating.

Joseph Forepaugh

The loss of his mistress was causing Forepaugh crippling grief, but he also had to deal with the scorn of the harshly judging social community in which he belonged. Perhaps it was the relentless guilt from his betrayal—or the deep pain his broken heart inflicted—but whatever the reason, he knew he had to act, and act he did. On the morning of Friday, July 9, 1892, distraught over the loss of his love, Forepaugh left his home without telling anyone of his destination or intention. For quite some time his family had noticed his erratic behavior and feared he was in a terrible state of mind. When he did not return home by supper, fearing the worst, the family organized a search party in order to retrieve him before something bad happened. As night encroached, the party had no choice but to postpone the search until the following morning. The next day the search was renewed, and shortly after 11am, Forepaugh's lifeless body was discovered along the Milwaukee railway tracks. The *St. Paul Pioneer Press* wrote that his body "lay on his right side at the foot of a tree, a revolver held in his right hand and a bullet wound in the right side of his head." The paper went on to suppose that "Mr. Forepaugh must have sat down at the foot of the tree, and after firing the fatal shot, must have fallen over on his right side." Law enforcement agents determined the cause of death as suicide, noting that Forepaugh had obviously blown his brains out with a pistol. Some of the gorier of the accounts remarked that his cold hand still frozenly gripped the death-inducing pistol. Forepaugh was a well-known and respected member of the community, making news of his suicide spread even faster than most. The *Logansport Journal* went so far as to report that his death had "caused a sensation" throughout the community. With the absence of any suicide letter, the question of what truly drove Forepaugh to his death remained a mystery. The initial public perception painted a picture of financial ruin, forcing him to end his life rather than suffer the embarrassment and shame that poverty would bring upon his already tarnished family. These rumors were mostly caused by Forepaugh's irrational belief that his business holdings were in turmoil. This speculation was quickly squashed with the release of his will that left his entire estate, estimated at nearly $500,000, to his wife. With the bankruptcy rumors put to rest, scintillating tales began swirling that Molly was pregnant with Forepaugh's illegitimate child. This, too, would remain an unsolved mystery—after Forepaugh's suicide, Molly grabbed a rope, headed up to the third floor, and joined her lover in the afterlife.

> # FOUND DEAD.
>
> ## A Retired St. Paul Capitalist Takes His Own Life.
>
> St. Paul, July 11.—J. L. Forepaugh, formerly of the firm of Forepaugh &

A 1892 newspaper article detailing Forepaugh's suicide

The suicide not only brought death to Forepaugh and his mistress, it also ushered in the downfall of his beloved mansion. With each passing year, the house fell deeper in to disrepair. Eventually, the mansion became so dilapidated that it had to be closed down when it was ruled unfit for human occupation. In 1974, the once grand Victorian home was about to be reborn. The home was painstakingly gutted and completely renovated to be used as a restaurant. It is believed that the construction not only brought the home back to life, but also the spirits of those who once occupied it. Forepaugh's Restaurant is consistently touted as a fine dining experience and every year thousands of guests visit the restaurant to enjoy a delicious meal. However, many unsuspecting guests tend to get a bit more than they had perhaps bargained for.

Silverware and plates are often moved by some unseen force

When I first investigated the restaurant in 2005, I was taken aback by the sheer number of experiences that both the staff and customers were reporting. One of the more common reports came from customers who, while enjoying a meal, often caught the sight of a ghostly man walking through the dining area. What I found fascinating about these accounts was the strikingly similar observations that described the physical details of the ghost. Most people stated that the ghost was an arrogant looking "man" who was strutting around the place as though he owned it. Of course, if it was the ghost of Joseph Forepaugh, he does own the place—or at least he did when he was alive. The sight of the wandering spirit is short lived, as he eventually walks into a wall and disappears. Many have come away with the impression that the ghost was Joseph Forepaugh, but he is not the only spirit lingering in the historic home. I interviewed several staff members who recalled their frequent encounters with something abnormal while inside the restaurant. On several occasions the workers would catch a brief glimpse of a woman brushing by them, yet when they would turn to gather a better look, the woman would have simply vanished into thin air. For years these sightings persisted, and no one spoke of their individual sightings for fear of what their co-workers might think. It wasn't until customers also began to report seeing the vanishing woman that the staff finally felt comfortable enough to share their own encounters. Much like the Forepaugh sightings, there are several similarities that exist among the many various reports of the woman. Most people report that the phantom looks as though she is from a previous time period. She is mainly spotted wearing a Victorian garb that would be more fitting of someone living in the late 1800s or early 1900s. The other off-putting thing about the woman is that she appeared to be nearly transparent, puzzling witnesses who could almost see right through her. The witnesses I spoke with believed that the strange looking woman was actually the ghost of young Molly. This odd theory gains some plausibility when you consider that the most haunted spot of Forepaugh's is the third floor chandelier—the very area where Molly was said to have taken her own life. If you are looking to break from mundane restaurant experiences, you can actually eat at a table that is directly under the notorious chandelier. Be warned—those who are seated there regularly report seeing the chandelier sway back and forth on its own, as though something is hanging from it. Most of the witnesses are oblivious to the fact that something—or should I say someone—did in fact hang from there. Some witnesses have even gone so far as to report hearing the odd sound of rope creaking from under the chandelier. Of course, these guests had no idea that Molly picked out the rope as her preferred method of suicide. In fact, so many odd things have taken place on the third floor that many employees refuse to work alone upstairs at night. Several workers informed me that they would rather be fired than work alone at night on the third floor.

The chandelier marks the area where Molly killed herself

Those with a squeamish stomach need not worry about forgoing the restaurant, as not all the paranormal activity at Forepaugh's is frightening. In fact, many of the spirits haunting the place have exhibited a playful side as well. I collected the following series of miscellaneous events. Taken on their own, they would not cause one to run in terror, however, when they are compiled together with other bizarre happenings, the prospect of finding yourself alone at Forepaughs quickly losses its appeal. I also spoke with a long time employee who told me of a bizarre experience that took place while she was busy doing her cleaning routine. She had just stopped at the coat closet to straighten up all of the empty hangers, spending a few seconds to make sure that all the hangers were equally spaced out from one another. When she finished the task, she turned around to leave and heard the sounds of the hangers clanging up against one another. When she spun around, she was amazed to discover that all of the hangers had been moved to one side of the closet. Assuming that the spirits wanted the hangers to stay that way, the woman quickly headed off toward a different area of the restaurant. The spirits also like to play with the restaurant's lighting. On numerous occasions the lights can be seen turning on and off as though controlled by something unseen. The story gets even stranger when employees routinely come to work only to discover that the dining chairs have been moved, rearranged, and even flipped upside down by some unknown force. Silverware that had been put out the night before a big event also has been found rearranged, almost as if someone had apparently disapproved of their placement and wanted to make sure everything was in its perfect place.

I also discovered that, like many other haunted places I have investigated, Forepaugh's Restaurant has been home to many unexplained cold spots. Several of the staff reported that while cleaning up at night they would walk into a cold patch of air, the cause of which could never be determined. It happened so frequently that the staff eventually just chalked it up as another bizarre Forepaugh's event and continued on with their jobs. It is interesting to note that paranormal researchers tend to believe that these artificial cold spots indicate the presence of a spirit, while skeptics claim that cold spots are nothing more than our overactive imaginations hard at work. With such a wide variety of paranormal events transpiring at Forepaugh's Restaurant, it is become increasingly difficult to disagree with those who believe that Forepaugh and Molly are still carrying on their ill-fated love affair . . . even from the grave.

I guess the only way to truly find out is to visit Forepaugh's Restaurant for yourself—and don't forget to ask for the table under the chandelier.

The Drowning of Charlotte Mills

Location:

Bridge over Black River
County Road H
Christie, WI

Haunting:

October is a transitional time of year when the cold starts to tighten its grip on us, the leaves wither and begin to rustle, and the once plentiful daylight gives way to more eerie darkness. It is a time when every bone-chilling breeze seems to act as a harbinger of troublesome things to come. Yet despite all of these imperfections, October is often cited by many as their favorite time of year, but for Charlotte Mills, October brought with it only heartache, misfortune, and death.

For years, the Mills family lived a perfectly happy and normal life in the small town of Christie, Wisconsin. Charlotte's first taste of October's cruel curse happened in 1901 when she received terrible news from Alaska that her oldest son Fay had drowned while working on a streamer that got caught in a fierce storm. The date of Fay's death was October 12th. Almost a year later, on October 2nd, the curse struck again . . . this time taking the life of Charlotte's son Benjamin, who died while working in Idaho. The deaths of her two sons weighed heavily on Charlotte who took comfort and solace in knowing that at least she was still blessed with a husband, and her youngest son, Claude. Unfortunately, death was not finished with the Mills family, because in 1905 her husband, John Calvin Mills, died suddenly of heart failure inside the family home. The death of her husband, compounded by those of her sons, placed too great a burden on Charlotte, causing her to sink into a spiral of depression. As the months went by, Charlotte did her best to hold the depression at bay. In 1907, the October curse came back for one last victim—Charlotte. On October 4th, Charlotte told Claude that she was heading off to visit her nearby friend. It was her usual custom to spend the night at her friend's home, so Claude thought nothing of it when his mother failed to return home that evening. The next morning still brought no word from Charlotte, causing a worried Claude to set off in search of her. The *Neillsville Times* wrote, "No one knowing her whereabouts, he searched for her, found tracks on the bank of the Black River, and after further search found her body floating in three feet of water." A brief and preliminary examination of Charlotte's lifeless body was performed by District Attorney Crosby and Dr. E.L. Bradbury. The men determined that the cause of death was so apparent that no inquest would be necessary. Further proof that the drowning was no accident was revealed when Claude discovered that prior to leaving, his mother had carefully placed on her bed the clothing that she desired to be buried in. Apparently Charlotte's woes had been building for quite some time. The *Neillsville Times* wrote that Charlotte "had been depressed for some time before and told her son that there was no use living, because of bad luck."

Frightened By Ghosts.

Albert Neis of Christie told th
police of Neillsville a peculiar tal
of spirits and specters, and is born

A 1907 newspaper article described the ghostly activity taking place on the bridge

In most situations, the tragic story of Charlotte's death would have slowly faded from public memory, eventually becoming nothing more than a sad tale told among the Mills' family lore. However, soon after Charlotte's death, strange things began taking place near the bridge where she had taken her life. On December 20th, the *La Crosse Tribune* carried the bizarre story of local resident, Albert Neis, who told the Neillsville Police "a peculiar tale of spirits and specters." Mr. Neis was returning home one evening when his horse inexplicably started to run away. At the exact same moment, a "brilliant v-shaped light rose up before him and then disappeared." Neis was convinced that the light was some sort of paranormal occurrence somehow connected to Charlotte's death. Another local man, Lenwood Shaw, also experienced the mysterious light darting around the old bridge. Shaw and his wife were returning from town when "the light rose at the approach of the bridge across the Black River." After being seen by three credible witnesses, it didn't take long for the tale of the mysterious light to reach the surrounding communities. The December 27th edition of the *Eau Claire Leader* claimed the "subject is being discussed in almost every household in that neighborhood." By the end of 1907, the light had made its baffling appearance to no less than eight traveling farmers. The overwhelming belief was that the light was caused by the ghost of Charlotte Mills, who was haunting the location of her death. The *Marshfield Times* claimed, "Superstitious persons attach much significance to the fact that Mrs. Mills drowned in the Black river this last fall." Soon, area farmers were doing everything they could to avoid crossing the bridge at night, stating that often times their horses simply refused to cross the bridge . . . as though they were picking up on something frightening that was not visible to the naked eye. Eventually the fear of the bridge began to dissipate, helped by the construction of a new, more modern bridge, and farmers tentatively returned to their old habits. And although no longer covered by the newspapers, sporadic encounters with the odd light continued.

As you just read, the abovementioned stories were all from the year 1907. Nearly one hundred years later, while researching old newspaper accounts for the book *Hidden Headlines of Wisconsin*, I stumbled upon this case and began speaking about it at conferences and lectures. I quickly discovered that although the origin of the story had been long forgotten, the paranormal happenings were still occurring. In 2004, a woman heard a radio interview I was doing on Charlotte's ghost and decided to share the story of what happened to her at the bridge. In 2002, the woman and her son decided to go fishing down by the bridge. Here is what she wrote:

> I had gone fishing 2 years ago and something very weird happened that day. The water was VERY low under the bridge, in fact the lowest I'd ever seen it there, so, we decided to stop there because we could walk by foot where you normally wouldn't be able to because the water was so low. We parked the truck and he stayed near the bridge fishing, but I walked a down a way south of the bridge. (He stayed fishing by the bridge for 15 minutes or so, while I was down further just messing around practicing casting over and over). Then I thought I saw 'something' and kept blinking my eyes because it looked 'blurry' and I wasn't sure if I saw a person in the distance by the water or not. I rubbed my eyes and blinked several times, then, couldn't see the person anymore. And I wasn't sure why, but, I got a really creepy feeling come over me, and I felt very uncomfortable being there. Then my son was walked toward me and asked what I was looking at and I said I wasn't sure but I thought I saw somebody or something. I don't think he was really aware that I was that feeling spooked, but, I felt very uneasy. We didn't say much to each other, and he kept fishing, but, I stopped casting completely and kind of just watched him but kept looking around and over my shoulders a lot. Finally, I just told him let's go, and he agreed, so we both walked back to the bridge together. After we got to the bridge, he cast a few more times and then out of the blue he made a comment about it feeling creepy there and he didn't want to fish there anymore. I wanted to

tell you about this because I'd never heard anything about the story of Charlotte Mills suicide you told until tonight.

Needless to say, October is a popular time for legend trippers to visit the bridge, hoping that the anniversary of Charlotte's death will help spark some paranormal activity. Without fail, each year produces a couple of reports from those who claim to have seen odd lights dancing around the bridge. For my own investigations, I have visited the bridge on numerous occasions. In order to hopefully encounter the mysterious light, I have visited the bridge on the anniversary of Charlotte's death, during many cold December nights, and throughout the mosquito infested summer months. One of the first things that struck me was the irony that an area with such a beautiful rural landscape could be offset with a truly awful history. Each of my investigations ended in disappointment. I did not see the mysterious ball of light, I did not capture odd photos or unexplained voices, and I did not come face to face with Charlotte's ghost. Yet for some unknown reason, this case continues to intrigue me. Perhaps the fascination rests in the whole slew of unanswered questions that I still hold about this legend. Alone, sitting in the darkness of the bridge, I couldn't help but wonder why Charlotte chose the Black River as her place of demise. Surely there are countless other less painful ways of meeting death. Even the act of self-drowning—fighting the body's natural response to survive—would take incredible will power... the same will power that Charlotte was unfortunately unable to garner in her quest to continue living.

Wayne's Red Apple Inn

Location:

32711 Michigan Ave.
Wayne, MI 48184
(734) 722–4100

Haunting:

Motels are not inherently scary places, but thanks to movies like Psycho, Vacancy, and Hostel, Hollywood has created the fear of spending the night in an unknown place. As kids we all hear, and even tell, the terrible tales of death and dismemberment that take place in secluded motels. In most cases, these wild stories are nothing more than standard urban legends circulated by teenagers and perhaps Holiday Inn executives. However, in Wayne, the Red Apple Inn has gained a dark reputation for being haunted due to many cases of tragedy and death that have taken place there. Although no one has been killed inside the motel, you may want to watch out if you plan to eat some pizza or consummate your wedding at the motel.

Over the years, several unusual deaths have taken place at the motel

If you search for the Red Apple haunted legend online, you will uncover numerous sites all claiming that much of the unexplained activity happens inside room 117. The motel owner told me that the legend of room 117 had been circulating for years, although the origin of the story is not known. Several times each year he is contacted by ghost research groups looking to spend the night in the room in hopes of capturing evidence of the playful ghost. Most believe that the room is haunted by a mischievous spirit who likes to hide items, move guests' personal belongings, and create knockings and other odd noises inside the room. One of the more popular legends of room 117 is the story of the death of a man named Charles "Chick" McGee. Legends states that Chick was a guest at the Red Apple Inn and decided to walk through the parking lot to grab a bite to eat at the nearby Red Apple Restaurant. Later that evening, Chick was found stabbed to death, his lifeless body covered in blood inside room 117. The murder case was never solved, but it was rumored that Chick was killed by an angry restaurant waitress who was stiffed on her tip. Chick's ghost now is said to hide the TV remote and is blamed for shampoo, soap, and other items being moved and hidden throughout the room. As farfetched as the story sounds, it has been posted on numerous ghost research sites as the gospel truth. I found no evidence of anyone being murdered inside the hotel. It is also an odd coincidence that the name Charles "Chick" McGee is the name of a permanent character on the widely popular Bob & Tom Show, a national radio program that is known for its hijinks.

Room 117 is thought to be one of the most haunted rooms at the motel

Perhaps the Chick story has been changed or mistaken from the real murder that occurred in the parking lot of where the Red Apple Inn now sits. According to the *Wayne Eagle* newspaper on July 21, 1968, Lamont Haack was pulling out of his parking space when a man threw a punch at him. Haack, a large man, jumped out of his car to confront the man, and was subsequently attacked by a group of seven to nine other men. While Haack was on the ground he was repeatedly kicked and punched by the men. Two outside witnesses came to his aid, but they were beaten back by the group. Later that night, Haack succumbed to his injuries. Witnesses reported that the assailants escaped in a Red Ford Torino and a 1964 Cadillac Convertible. The case remains unsolved. Perhaps it is the spirit of Haack who haunts the area where he lost his life. But Haack wasn't the only one to die on the property, as the Inn has been home to several strange deaths over the years. A few years back, a married couple had booked room 221 for the night and requested some privacy. Later that night their privacy ended when an ambulance was called to the room. When the paramedics arrived, they found out that the wife had died while having sex with her husband.

Over the years, the number of deaths at the motel began to add up. The Wayne Historical Museum told me the story of a woman who died from a heroin overdose while staying at the hotel in 1997. In 2008, two more guests met death during their stay at the inn. One unlucky man was found dead in his room after he apparently choked to death on the pizza he was eating, while yet another guest was found dead in his room from a drug overdose.

Don't feel bad if room 117 is not available for your stay, because numerous guests staying in other rooms have reported strange activity as well. There have been countless guests that report hearing unusual knockings on the walls and other mysterious noises coming from inside their rooms. Others complain of clothing and other personal items being moved by some unseen hand. While the overwhelming majority of people staying at the inn have no problem with its grisly past, some would rather not stay at a motel where some guests never check out.

Bootlegging and Bloodshed
St. Paul, Minnesota

Bootlegging and Bloodshed

Location:

215 Wabasha St. S
Saint Paul, MN
(651) 224–1191
www.wabashastreetcaves.com

Haunting:

Although now mostly hidden by time and development, the series of caves indented into the landscape along Wabasha Street played an important role in the lives of many Minnesotans. Unfortunately, due to vandalism and several accidental deaths, many of the caves in the area have been sealed up to be forever forgotten. Yet the Wabasha Street Caves business is still open to the public, and it remains a constant reminder of the place's sorted past.

During the early 1900s, the unique combination of the caves being cool, dark, and damp places merged to create the perfect environment for the growing of mushrooms. In fact, the conditions were so suited to mushroom growing, that the Wabasha Street Caves soon became the leading producer of mushrooms in the entire United States. The caves were also plentiful with silica, which was swiftly mined out of the caves in order to produce glass needed to help feed the young booming automobile market. However, it was during prohibition that the owners discovered that the expansive caves could also accommodate a whiskey still. Cave number seven was chosen to house the main whiskey still, a decision that would forever alter the fate of the caves. Word about the quality still quickly spread, and soon thirsty citizens from all over the Twin Cities were visiting the caves for a tasty sip of the illegal brew. The place "unofficially" opened and was simply called the Wabasha Street Speakeasy. It served as an underground meeting place where the public could spend the night eating, dancing, drinking, and gambling. It was also the type of place where a man could go to partake in the comfort of one of the "ladies of the night" that made their living working at the speakeasy.

Of course, while the speakeasy gladly catered to the inhibitions of the community, it also opened the door for many unsavory characters to wander in. During this time period St. Paul was a safe haven for many of the nation's most infamous gangsters and crooks. The caves were a favorite nighttime hangout for noted criminals like George "Baby Face" Nelson, Alvin "Creepy" Karpis, Homer Van Meter, the deadly Barker Gang, and a plethora of other dangerous characters. It was at the caves where a young lady attending a dance got a little closer to danger than she could have ever intended. Legend states that it happened in the early 1930s when the caves were still an illegal operation. The speakeasy often hired big bands to entertain their clientele, and one evening a young woman was listening to the wonderful sounds of the big band when a stranger approached her and asked for a dance. Being that this was the1930s, the woman normally would not have accepted an invitation to dance from a complete stranger, but there was something about this man's glowing confidence that really intrigued her. After some thought she hesitantly agreed to a dance, and when they were finished dancing the man left with several of his buddies. Immediately several of her friends rushed over to her side and said, "Do you know who were just dancing with?" A bit confused by all of the attention, the young woman replied, "No, but I wished he would have stayed because he was a great dancer." The woman's excitement climbed even higher when she was told that her mysterious dance partner was the most wanted man in the world—John Dillinger.

Once that it was certain that prohibition was coming to an end, the cave owners, William and Josie Lehmann, set about transforming the place into a legal nightclub, and in 1933 the Castle Royal nightclub officially opened its doors. Even though the establishment was then legal in the eyes of the law, the place could not shake some of their shady clientele. These underworld men ensured that the former speakeasy often reared its dark and deadly side. In 1934, four of the club's patrons were gathered around a table where they were involved in a heated game of poker. It was late at night, and the cleaning woman thought it was weird that all of the men had music cases with them, even though none of them played in a band. As the woman was tending to her duties, she heard the sound of machine gun fire blasting through the caves. When she ran back to see what had transpired, she was horrified to discover that three of the men had been mowed down, while the fourth man was perfectly fine. She immediately called for the St. Paul Police who arrived and took control of the situation. The police told the shaken woman not to worry, that they would take care of everything. The police got right to work on the crime scene, and after about an hour had passed, the police called the woman back to the area of the alleged murders. The woman expected the police to ask her what had happened, but instead she was threatened with a harsh warning for playing games and wasting their valuable time. Looking around, the woman was shocked to discover that the place was completely spotless; the police had cleaned up the entire area. The official police response was that nothing had happened . . . it was all in the imagination of the overworked woman. The woman distinctly recalled that the bloody bodies of the three dead men were not taken from the caves that day; instead the employee believed the bodies were buried somewhere deep into the back end of the caves. Although everyone knew the St. Paul Police were corrupt, no one believed this young woman's story, except for the fact that she had physical proof: a series of bullet holes from the gunfire were lodged into the stone above the fireplace. To this day the stray bullet holes can still be seen above the fireplace, serving as a constant reminder of the caves' deadly secrets.

Evidence of a gunfight still remains in the wall

The Most Gruesome Hauntings of the Midwest

In the 1970s, disco fever was sweeping through the United States. The Casino Royal nightclub had fallen victim to the trend, and hosted many disco music laced parties. One evening, while closing up after a long night of business, the manager and an employee spotted a strange man walk right by them. Certain that no one could have gotten into the locked up establishment, the two baffled men carefully watched the stranger as he walked right into a cave wall and disappeared. To make matters even more confusing, the witnesses stated that the mysterious visitor was dressed like a gangster from the 1920s. The two men were unable to account for what had transpired and thought that maybe they were losing their minds. However, the men could take solace in the fact that when it came to seeing phantom gangsters lingering inside the caves, they were certainly not alone. One day the owners were inside the caves with their young son. While his parents were engaged in various cleaning and maintenance duties, the boy was aimlessly bouncing a tennis boy around the caves. On one bounce, the ball got away from him and traveled into the men's restroom, finally coming to a stop near the mirror. The energetic young boy bent down to retrieve the ball, and when he stood back up and gazed into the mirror, he was startled to see a gangster looking man standing right behind him. Confused, the boy twirled around, and much to his amazement, the gangster was nowhere to be found.

Restroom where a lot of paranormal activity takes place

Perhaps the most infamous gangster encounter happened during one of the numerous weddings that take place inside the caves. Due to the elegant beauty and colorful history of the place, many love-stricken couples decide to hold their ceremonies inside the naturally cooled walls of the caves. On one such occasion, a large wedding party was winding down toward the end of the reception. As guests were starting to depart, one young boy commented that he really enjoyed playing with all of the funny gangsters who were at the party. The members of the wedding party thought that the boy, like most other boys his age, simply had a good imagination and had made up the story to help pass away the time. A few days later, while looking through the developed wedding photos, the newlyweds discovered that one of the photos showed a strange mist hovering near the young boy. Convinced that the mist was evidence of the phantom gangster, the couple sent the photo back to the caves, where curious visitors today can still view it and come to their own conclusion as to whether phantom gangsters still enjoy a night out at the caves.

It should be noted that more than just phantom gangsters are reported to roam the inner tunnels of the street caves. One spirit in particular seems to have a mischievous side to it. Many staff members report that while working in the back section of the caves, they will often hear their name being called out, yet when they attempt to respond, no one can be found. Other staff members talk of being pushed or pinched by some unseen force while wandering through the caves. Both employees and tour goers have caught glimpses of strange glowing globes of light floating through the bar area of the caves. These small orbs can be spotted changing in both color and size, and many of the unknown lights have appeared in the pictures taken of the caves.

Cave leading to the old whiskey still

The versatile caves have also been home to several theatrical plays throughout the years. It is during these high-usage times that the paranormal activity appears to blossom. During several different productions actors, immersed in rehearsals, have looked off stage and spotted the faint image of a bus boy casually leaning on the side of a table, as though he was taking a quick rest while enjoying the show. Yet without fail, the phantom bus boy is almost always reported to disappear into thin air. On another night, a group of seven actors were up on stage with the director performing a scene from their upcoming performance. Although the caves were completely empty, the group swore they had seen a ghostly image of a man sitting at a table reserved for the audience. The identity of this phantom critic was never determined.

Adding even more mystery to the already spooky caves are the numerous stories coming from those taking the historic caves tour, who report getting more entertainment than they have paid for. Some lucky (or unlucky) visitors taking the guided tour have split off from the main group, either to use the restrooms, or take a moment to gain a closer look at some of the photos decorating the caves, only to hear the muffled sounds of a 1930s era big band starting up. At first thought the visitors think that the tour includes the music of a big band. It is not until they rejoin the group that they realize that there is no band playing that day, and the beautiful music they heard was not provided on the tour. The spectral sounds have been heard drifting through the caves by so many people that they are thought to be some ghostly remnants of the big band musicians that used to play the night away back in the heyday of the caves.

Of course, no haunted case would be complete without the eyewitness accounts of psychics. As with any tourist location that attracts loads of people, some of them are going to be intuitives, or mediums. Every once in a while an unsuspecting medium will show up for a cave tour without knowing anything about the haunted reputation of the place. Inevitably, these mediums end up asking the staff if the place is haunted. One cave, towards the end of the tour, seems to be a hotbed of paranormal activity. In a relativity small area, many people have seen the spirit of an unknown woman lingering around. During one cave tour, when the group reached the haunted area, a medium that was in the group stated that she was picking up on the restless spirit of a woman in the area. The tour guide then confirmed that the very area they were standing was the spot where people had not only seen the unknown woman, they had even captured her spirit on their cameras.

So what is the cause behind all of the unexplainable activity that occurs at the caves? Could it be that the souls of those men killed in a botched card game still wander the caves seeking eternal peace? It is possible that the spirit of an unidentified woman haunts curious visitors? Does the music of former big bands still echo the halls of the caves? The truth is that no one is completely certain why the caves are so haunted. One thing we do know is that if you want to come face to face with the ghosts of fallen gangsters, there is no better place to do it than in St. Paul.

Villisca Axe Murder House

Villisca, Iowa

Villisca Axe Murder House

Location:

Villisca Axe Murder House
508 East 2nd Street
Villisca, IA 50864
(712) 621–1530
www.villiscaiowa.com

Haunting:

Many people profess an aversion to non-chain "mom and pop" motels. Mainly this dislike is fueled by Hollywood's never ending parade of bad movies that portray roadside motels as incubators for killers, criminals, kidnappers, and rapists. Most intriguing is that while general middle of the road Americans tend to avoid this type of lodging, fearing that perhaps someone was murdered there, the Axe Murder House—where people were actually murdered—attracts throngs of eager customers who willing to pay top dollar to see if they are brave enough to spend the night. One of the most common questions I receive is from people who want to know of a haunted location where they can spend the night. If you share a similar macabre sense of adventure, the Villisca Axe Murder House a must visit stop.

Little has changed at the home since 1912

On June 10, 1912, the little sleepy town of Villisca got a horrific wake-up call. The town was abuzz with talk regarding the horrible events of the previous night's murders. As word spread through town, residents could not believe that they had a murderer among them. The town's disbelief quickly changed when investigators arrived at the scene and found the farm house chalk full of bludgeoned bodies. The murders took place as Josiah Moore, his wife Sarah, and their children Herman, Katherine, Boyd, and Paul were returning home for the evening. Thanks to a severe case of bad timing, the Moore children had invited their two friends Lena and Ina Stillinger to spend the night. With what now are considered primitive means of investigation, officers believe that the killer (or killers) might have been hiding inside the home waiting for the Moore family to return. As soon as the family turned in for the night, the killer pounced, moving from room to room ending the lives of each person as his axe left a bloody trail of destruction. The neighing of the Moore's horses alerted neighbors who reported to police that no activity was noticed from the usually busy family. The bodies were discovered sometime between 8am and 8:30am, and foolishly only one deputy was charged with securing the crime scene. When word of the murders got out, many curious and frightened townsfolk bypassed the guard and entered through one of the three doors leading into the house. The crime scene was a complete zoo; residents were tracking blood throughout the house, neighbors stole items to keep as souvenirs, and a local pool hall owner by the name of Bert McCaull was said to have taken a piece of Moore's skull back to his business wrapped in yellow paper. According to the *Emporia Gazette*, the murder weapon, an axe "covered with blood and hair" was discovered leaning against a basement wall. Investigators believed that the killer saw the Moore adults as the biggest threats and therefore made sure to kill them first, smashing them with his axe as they slept in their front room bed. With the parents out of the picture, evidence suggests that the killer then moved to another room where he bashed in the heads of the four Moore children so severely that newspapers reported that all that remained of the children was a pile of pulp. Finally, the killer encountered the two sisters who were sleeping together in their own room. With the blood-drenched axe he nearly took off the girls' heads. The *Mansfield News* wrote "Owning to the terrible mutilation the identity of the two women could not at first be established." Dr. J. Clark Cooper, the coroner that worked on the case, reported that the bodies of the dead children were all found faced down towards the bed. Newspaper reports stated that all of the children were still tucked into bed and their bedcovers remained undisturbed. Other odd things seemed out of place for a murder too… a mirror had been covered up with a bedspread, the faces of the victims were covered with bedcovers or discarded clothes, and all of the curtains had been pulled shut. Police ruled out the possibility of the murder being a robbery gone bad, because none of the family's jewelry or money were taken. The only thing police were certain of was that eight people were dead, and the killer remained loose.

One of the rooms where the murders took place

The Main Suspects:

Even though the case has been documented in excruciating detail in several books, documentary videos, and numerous websites, the case has never been fully solved. Even though no one was ever convicted of the brutal murders, there were plenty of named suspects, including:

Reverend George Kelly—Rev. Kelly was a traveling preacher who settled down in Iowa in 1912. In 1917, Rev. Kelly was arrested and charged with the murder. Even with an alleged confession (that was later retracted) the trial ended in a hung jury. Convinced that they had found their man, Kelly was re-tried, this time he fared much better and was acquitted. Most of the evidence of the case surrounded the fact that Kelly showed up in Villisca for a church event the day of the murders and then abruptly left the following morning.

Frank Jones—Frank was Josiah Moore's boss for several years until Josiah left his job to start his own implement company. When he left, Josiah took with him a very profitable John Deere franchise contract. Witnesses stated that Jones was visibly upset about the betrayal. It didn't help his cause that it was rumored that Moore was having an affair with Jones' daughter-in-law. Rumors spread and Jones was accused of hiring a hit man to kill Moore, yet Jones was never arrested or charged and adamantly denied any involvement in the crime.

William Mansfield—Mansfield was the hit man that was said to be hired by Frank Jones. Obviously, Mansfield's reputation as a cocaine-addicted serial killer didn't help his cause either. Add in the speculation that he was responsible for the axe murder of his own wife and family and Mansfield becomes the perfect suspect. Unlike many of the other suspects, he was actually arrested but later released due to the lack of evidence against him. Mansfield's name was cleared when he was awarded over $2,000 in a lawsuit ensuing from his wrongful arrest.

Miscellaneous—Residents of the town also put forth their own theories including a traveling serial killer, a hobo, and even a crazed maniac. None of these far-fetched theories ever panned out, however, as the case is still unsolved.

The Haunting:

The Villisca Axe Murder house may be the most investigated home in all of Iowa. Numerous paranormal research groups from around the country have traveled to Villisca in hopes of gathering evidence of the home's haunted activity. The list of reported phenomenon at the home is nearly endless, and while we may never known the full extent of the evil that was committed on that fateful night, the weathered home seems to be more than willing to share its secrets. The home is open to the general public for both daily tours and nightly sleepovers. When I spoke with the former owner (now deceased) he told me that over the years he had come to believe that the home was truly haunted by its past. During tours, visitors have reported seeing furniture moving on its own, hearing unknown voices, seeing lamps that refuse to stay on, and spotting unknown shadowy figures moving through the house. The owner also told me the story of a young boy who was visiting the home with his father. Something about the old home had sparked the boy's curiosity and he began to wander through the rooms, eventually finding himself upstairs. When he came back downstairs he told his father that a strange man upstairs had touched him. Knowing that they were alone in the house, the father wondered who could have touched his son. The boy looked upstairs as though he was looking at someone standing there, pointed to the staircase and said, "He did." The confused father looked at the staircase but saw no one.

Those who are looking for a more intimate experience with the home's spirits may want to consider spending the night inside the home. If you go online, you can listen to recordings from various groups that have claimed that while they were investigating the home they were able to capture the ghostly voices (EVP) of the dead children, the killer, and even Josiah and Sarah Moore. Others who are brave enough to spend the night report a vast assortment of weird activity that took place during their stay. Photos taken inside the home are often filled with unusual balls of light (orbs) that were not seen with the naked eye. Believe it or not, many visitors actually are able to fall asleep while staying at the home, and many of them have reported feeling a strong pressure on their chest as through something was sitting directly on top of them. The old home also has had problems with doors that open and close on their own; this most frequently occurs with the door to the room where the Moore children were murdered. More bizarre reports of activity in the house revolve around several visitors that had seen what appeared to be blood dripping from the walls. However, when the shocked witnesses tried to investigate the mysterious phenomenon, they discovered that the blood was simply gone.

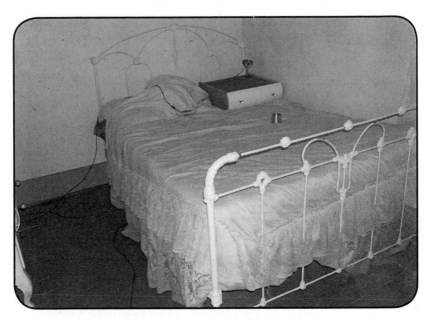

Sleeping accommodations inside the home

Psychics also frequent the home hoping that their skills may lend some help in the investigation. They claim that when they call out to the children they are often pushed, pinched, or shoved by some unseen force. One visitor was hanging out upstairs and had sat down on the bed and started calling out for a response from one of the children when all of a sudden he felt a tug on his pant leg. He looked under the bed to find the source of the tug, but was shocked to find nothing under the bed.

In 2009, I received this email from a gentleman who visited the home with his wife, and the two of them ended up getting a bit more than they had bargained for:

> I am from Missouri but only live about 10–15 miles from the Iowa border. About two years ago, me and my wife visited the Villisca Axe Murder house as we found it very intriguing. We took many pictures but nothing really showed up paranormal in them. But we did have a couple of personal experiences. While we were downstairs in the living room, Darwin Linn told the history of the house and the murders. Later, my wife told me that she felt something like a bug on her neck but when she felt it, there was nothing there. I also felt my

back getting very cold as I stood in a downstairs bedroom doorway. When I felt my shirt, it wasn't cold. But my back underneath was! After I had the cold feeling, Darwin explained in his story that right where I was standing was where the axe that committed the murders was found!

The most gruesome happening inside the home comes in the re-creation of the murders that are played out by the spirits. The spirits of the home are mainly thought to be of those unfortunate souls who were brutally murdered there. Yet, on several occasions, witnesses have claimed to see a deranged looking man going from room to room while carrying a bloody axe. Based on their accounts, it seems that the horrific crimes of June 10, 1912 have forever linked the murderer to the home as well.

The Witch's Grave
Chesterville, Illinois

The Witch's Grave

Location:

Chesterville Cemetery
Chesterville, IL

Haunting:

In the U.S., many small rural towns are saddled with a reputation of being places where nothing exciting ever happens. Teenagers seem to perpetually long for the perceived excitement and vibrancy that they think only exists in large cities. The countryside around the town of Chesterville is dotted with Amish and Mennonite communities who have spent decades working the fertile farming land, but electricity free farming does little to dispel the erroneous stereotype that all small towns are boring. One only has to partake in a bit of digging to discover that underneath the all the rural peacefulness, darker, more sinister legends are lurking in Chesterville.

One of the most widely known legends of the area is that of the vengeful witch that haunts the Chesterville Cemetery. According to local lore, years ago a young woman in the Amish community started to stray from the strict teachings of her elders and began to dabble in the dark art of witchcraft. With her new found sense of confidence, the woman soon began openly complaining about how women in her community were being unfairly treated. The tradition-minded elders were none too happy with her liberal thoughts and sought out to have her silenced. The elders started spreading fears among its members that the woman had made a pact with the Devil and was practicing satanic rituals. If this type of illicit behavior was allowed to continue it might threaten everyone by inviting evil spirits into to the close-knit community. After being caught performing a strange ritual, the woman mysteriously disappeared. A few days later, the woman's decomposing body was discovered in a nearby crop field. The elders used her 'unexplained' death as a grim warning to anyone looking to veer from their teachings. The body was placed on public display, and the elders kept close watch over her under fears that she may rise from the dead and take vengeance on her killers. After a few days, the woman was finally buried in the cemetery where her grave served as a constant reminder on the ills of witchcraft.

Touch the tree- if you dare

Another equally fascinating version of the story tells of the young woman as an accomplished healer who was equipped with supernatural powers allowing her to communicate with animals. Fearful that the woman was doing the Devil's bidding, the elders put an end to both her healing . . . and her life. Not knowing the true extent of the woman's metaphysical powers, the elders took every precaution they could think of in order to protect themselves from her spirit. With the dirt still fresh from her burial, a tree was planted directly over her grave with the belief that it would prevent her spirit from rising up from the dead. As an additional caution, they surrounded her grave with a heavy iron fence also meant to trap her spirit and prevent it from returning.

Over the years, the telling and re-telling of the legend have made the cemetery infamous among legend trippers looking to test their bravery and hopefully encounter some paranormal activity at a place now known unofficially as 'Witch Cemetery.' Little is known about the official history of the Chesterville Cemetery. Although many of the burial dates appear to be in the late 1800s, it doesn't seem to be as old as several other local cemeteries which have graves dating back to the 1830's and 1840's. In 2005, I traveled to Chesterville to see if I could dig up any additional information on this bizarre case. On my first day in town, I spoke with a local historian who informed me that the cemetery is not an Amish cemetery. A three-month-old girl with the last name of Harshbarger (an Amish name) was buried inside the cemetery in 1874, most likely because there wasn't an Amish cemetery established at the time of her death. The grave site of the alleged witch is located underneath a large looming oak tree, making it pretty simple to locate. Legend states that the tree is trapping the witch's spirit, and if anything were to happen to the tree, whether it be blown down in a storm or cut down, the witch's spirit would no longer be contained, and she would be free to seek revenge on the family of her killers. One of most lasting mysteries of the legend revolves around the question of the witch's real name. Outside of knowing that a female was buried in the grave, we know little about the identity of the witch. Unfortunately, the name of the grave's occupant has been lost to history, and no cemetery record of the grave has yet been located.

Grave location of suspected Witch

The fact that no one knows the real identity of the witch is just one of the many baffling aspects to this perplexing legend. While investigating the cemetery, I was told of a woman who took her daughter out to visit the cemetery only to vow that they would never do so again. It was a perfect day, the sun was shining, it wasn't too hot, and the birds even seemed to greet the duo with a series of lovely songs. As the mother slowly approached the witch's grave, everything started to change. Suddenly inexplicable feelings of anger and loneliness rushed over the mother as she fought to remain standing. The daughter wasn't immune from the strange sensations either, as she felt as though some unseen force was trying to push her out of the cemetery. Fearing for what might happen if they tempted fate and remained at the cemetery, the family swiftly set out for their car. Strangely, they noticed that the birds had stopped singing and the cemetery had taken on a morose silence.

By far, the most commonly reported activity at the cemetery is the frequent sightings of the witch herself. By modern standards, the cemetery is considered relatively small; from the middle of the grounds you can get a clear view of the entire place. Having an unimpeded view of the cemetery may account for so many people seeing the witch. One such witness told me that she was driving by the cemetery one evening when her eyes were drawn to a figure of a transparent woman standing next to the witch's grave. Certain that she had just caught a glimpse of the witch, the woman was too frightened to stop to put her theory to the test. Others have also seen what appears to be the glowing witch mournfully standing next to the very tree that eternally traps her spirit. In his book, *Weird Illinois*, researcher Troy Taylor included the story of a man who had grown up in the area who remembered an odd brush with the supernatural that occurred at the cemetery while he was in high school. While out on a run, the young man passed by the cemetery without so much as a second thought. On his return trip back, he noticed a woman staring at him while standing at the site of the witch's grave. Thinking it was someone fooling around with the grave he yelled out that the cemetery was closed. Much to his amazement, the mysterious woman let out a loud chuckle and then simply disappeared.

Grave under cursed tree

There are several key nuances of this case that separate it from the hundreds of mundane sightings of witches across the country. First is the inclusion of several burial procedures that were meant to ward off and contain evil spirits. Many cultures around the world subscribe to the belief that a tree planted over the grave will soak up the essence of the deceased spirit, thereby trapping them from coming back to haunt the living. The large old oak tree at Witch Cemetery certainly fits the description of a protective tree. The second part of the precautionary burial tricks involves the rickety old iron fence that was strategically placed around the grave of the witch. Most people wrongly assume that these types of fences and gates were placed there to keep people out. In actuality, many of the protective barriers were constructed to keep spirits in. Folkloric belief dictates that spirits are unable to pass through iron, so if you had wronged somebody in life and were afraid of them extracting revenge on you from the afterlife you would place an iron bar on their casket, or better yet, surround their grave with an iron gate. The final safety piece of Witch Cemetery is its location. The cemetery runs alongside the Okaw River, which is significant because much like Vampire lore, ghost lore contends that spirits cannot pass over running water. To offer protection from the dead, many communities would establish local cemeteries away from the village on the other side of running water. With all these protective measures, one has to wonder just what they were trying to protect themselves from.

The abovementioned barriers should be more than adequate to protect visitors from the witch's wrath, however, the dare at Witch Cemetery might just prove otherwise. The dare is that at midnight, if you are brave enough to run into the cemetery and touch the trunk of the tree, your disrespectful actions will anger the witch, and she will make herself known to you. It should be mentioned that midnight is not the only time strange things have occurred—one gentleman who was walking the cemetery discovered that the witch doesn't seem to follow any set routine. One day while leisurely strolling among the graves, the young man noticed the large oak tree and extended his hand toward the trunk, and as soon as contact was made, the young man's body went ice cold until his hand was removed from the tree.

Protective iron gate surrounding the grave

It is discouraging to me that there are so many various components of this case that remain unknown. Who is buried inside the witch's grave, how did she meet her fate, and was anyone responsible for her death? These unanswered questions are likely to continue to linger, bound forever to the legend itself. With little other evidence to gather, the one thing I took away from this case is that regardless of all the missing details surrounding the identity of the person buried inside the witch's grave, the fact still remains that the iron fence wasn't put up in order to keep us out.

The Cursed Washington Avenue Bridge

Location:

Washington Avenue Bridge
University of Minnesota
Minneapolis, MN

Haunting:

Most us give little thought to the deeper significance that bridges hold. In the physical world, bridges simply provide us with a means of crossing various bodies of water in order to reach our land-based destination.

Yet, in the metaphysical world, bridges are thought to take on a more significant role by acting as a link between the living and spiritual worlds. More importantly is the role of the water that rests beneath our man-made structures. Throughout history, numerous cultures have believed that running water acts as repellent to paranormal activity, some even suggesting that creatures such as vampires and ghosts are bound to the shoreline, unable to cross over running water. These ancient beliefs account for so many of our cemeteries being located near water. Years ago, when a person passed away, the community would bury their body on the other side of running water in order to prevent that person from coming back from the dead to seek revenge on those who wronged them in life. Throughout my years of research, I have encountered hundreds of stories of bridges being plagued by disembodied balls of lights, unexplained floating mist-like substances, and mysterious sightings of phantom spirits. So, when I first heard of the strange tales involving the Washington Avenue Bridge, I figured it would end up being just another run of the mill haunted bridge. But once I started my research, I quickly discovered that the bridge had a long and sorted history of tragedy. In fact, after gathering up many gruesome tales of death, I started to believe that the bridge may be some type of supernatural beacon that beckons out to those looking to end their lives—either by choice, or by chance.

In 1884, the expanding landscape of Minneapolis got a boost through the construction of an iron truss bridge connecting the east and west banks of the Mississippi River. Right from the start, the entire area seemed to be plagued with mishaps and never-ending safety concerns. In 1896, the *Freeborn County Standard* reported that Thomas Shafer, an 18-year-old boy, was out climbing some rocks near the bridge with some pals when he lost his footing, and plunged to his death. In 1911, the *Austin Daily Herald* wrote that Mart McDonald, a twenty-four-year-old taxi driver, lost control of his vehicle and smashed into the side rail of the bridge with such force that he was hurled over the hood of his car and plunged 100 feet into the water. Amazingly, when rescuers finally reached him, he was still alive and as they rushed his "horribly crushed" body to the city hospital where death soon ended his pain. By then, it seemed as though visits to the bridge from the Grim Reaper were becoming more and more frequent with no reprieve in sight. In June of 1913, the *Albert Lea Evening Tribune* told the ironic story of a distraught young 25-year-old waiter named George Kane who, after struggling with finances for so long, had found himself penniless and hopeless. Kane, who had grown tired of being distraught over his poverty, desperately craved release from his sense of failure as he walked to the side of the bridge and leapt to his watery grave. Unbeknownst to Kane, irony seemed to be playing a cruel joke on him. When they finally fished Kane's body out of the river, the authorities set out to notify his family. After being contacted by the morgue, the father revealed that he had spent the last two years searching for his wayward son in order to inform him that he had inherited over $40,000 from his deceased uncle's estate. Upon identifying the body of his lifeless son, the father's only words were "if only."

It should be noted that not all suicide attempts at the bridge actually end in death. Sometimes fate (or luck) has a strange way of showing itself, as evidenced by the bizarre case of Elsie Bassett who, in September of 1915, decided to end her own life. According to the *La Crosse Tribune,* Bassett, a library employee at the University, walked out to the bridge with the intentions of committing suicide and flung herself from the bridge. Bassett fell more than 90 feet before crashing into the cold churning waters of the Mississippi. Much to everyone's surprise —including her own—after hitting the water Basset found that she was in perfect condition and simply "swam ashore." With so many mishaps occurring on or near the bridge, whispers about the bridge being cursed began to pass from the lips of the locals. The bridge had already gone through an upgrade in 1890 that was intended to help alleviate some of the stress caused by increased public streetcar traffic when city officials began looking at other ways to improve the safety of the bridge as well. All of these preventative measures had little effect in diminishing the bridge's dark and deadly reputation—a reputation that was about to get even darker.

In April of 1920, the *Appleton Post Crescent* reported that police were searching the water under the bridge for "the body of a well dressed woman who was seen to leap from the Washington avenue bridge." It is not known if the authorities ever located the woman or if her body simply vanished. An even more bizarre incident took place six years later. William Carlson was out enjoying a stroll across the bridge with his wife when suddenly he inexplicably jumped over the railing and dove 100 feet to his instant death below, leaving his shocked wife on the bridge alone. The *La Crosse Tribune and Leader-Press* claimed that Mr. Carlson "had been ill for a year," so maybe he had planned the suicide well in advance. As the number of suicide victims at the bridge continued to climb, so did the freak accidents. In 1933, authorities discovered a pair of 100-foot-long rubber tire marks that ended at a gaping hole in the guard rail. Researchers assumed that someone had lost control of their car and plummeted over the side of the bridge. Later that day, their fears came true when the bodies of two young men were fished from the waters, the additional body of a woman riding along with them was never found.

Overlooking the river, the site is home to many suicides

Without witnesses, suicide letters, or other supporting evidence, the cause behind many bridge deaths remained unknown. In 1941, the *Brainerd Daily Dispatch* reported on one such case involving Fritz Clausen, whose body was recovered from the Mississippi River. Police were unable to determine whether Clausen jumped or fell from the bridge. Of course, they could also not rule out the possibility that perhaps Clausen was pushed from the bridge. As residents of the area debated the cause of the tragedies, the list of deadly occurrences continued to rise. In 1950, the body of Matt Stoke was found by an excavating crew working along the river. In 1951, the *Winona Republican-Herald* reported that "the body of a neatly dressed man" had been found near the east end of the bridge. Not willing to take any chances, the man had been so hell-bent on dying that he "slashed his wrists before jumping to his death." Tired of the ongoing accidents and suicides, the local residents began suggesting that a new bridge was needed to put an end to the deaths. In 1962, just downstream from the cursed old iron bridge, work began on a new bridge, and with the completion of the new bridge in 1965, the old bridge was finally torn down. Those who assumed that a new bridge would bring an end to the suicides were sorely mistaken.

The new double-decker bridge was a vast improvement over the previous death ridden bridge. The lower portion of the new bridge was used for vehicle traffic, while the upper deck provided plenty of room for students and pedestrians to safely cross the river. It also provided the opportunity for Peter Cashman, a U of M freshman, to fall to his death in 1970. Perhaps the most infamous suicide on the bridge occurred in 1972, when University Professor, and noted poet, John Berryman used the bridge to jump to his death. This is the point in time when the supernatural stories surrounding the bridge really began to spread. Those who were brave enough to cross over the bridge at night reported being overwhelmed with the feeling that someone (or something) was following behind them. Hurrying their step, the frightened pedestrians also noticed the sound of heavy footsteps encroaching upon them, even though no person could be found.

Phantom footsteps can be heard inside the walkway

After a lecture I gave in St. Paul, a U of M student approached me to tell of his encounter while crossing the bridge. Having spent several hours studying for a test, it was well into the wee hours of the night before the man headed home. The lateness of the hour ensured that few others were out moving around the area. As the man approached the bridge, an odd uneasiness began to build inside his body. With his senses peaked, sounds of heavy footsteps began to enclose in from behind him. But as soon as he stopped to listen, the footsteps were silenced, only to mysteriously start up again when the man continued on his way. Each and every time the man paused to look around, he found that he was all alone. The heavy footsteps continued to gain ground on him, forcing him to pick up his pace. He informed me that while racing through the final portion of the tunnel, he became convinced that he was not alone, believing that if he had not exited the bridge when he did, whatever was following him would have certainly caught him. What the young man didn't realize is that he was by no means alone in his odd experience. Each year I receive over a dozen reports of these odd phantom footsteps haunting the bridge. Although spectral footsteps are one thing, others report an even more bizarre experience. On several occasions, while passing over the bridge, witnesses have spotted someone preparing to jump over the side. Concerned that the stranger was about to commit suicide, the witnesses hurried over . . . only to see the "jumper" disappear right before their eyes.

Over the past twenty years, dozens of additional deaths have only added to the paranormal happenings on the bridge. One theory, subscribed to by many researchers, contends that powerful events—such as suicides or untimely accidents—leave an irreversible negative mark upon the land. This theory leads many to believe that the Washington Avenue Bridge is indeed haunted by the spirits of those who took their own life and are now are forced to spend eternity at the location where they sealed their doomed fate.

The Butcher of Plainfield
Plainfield, Wisconsin

The Butcher of Plainfield

Location:

Plainfield, WI
True Value Hardware Store—111 S. Main St.
Former Gein Farmstead
Plainfield Cemetery

Haunting:

Even those who are not familiar with the name Ed Gein probably are familiar with the Hollywood movies that are based on his gory actions. Movies like *Psycho, Texas Chain Saw Massacre, and Silence of the Lambs* all use Gein's demented personality as a basis for their sadistic characters. Most people think of Gein simply as a murderer, but his real passion in life was digging up the recently deceased bodies of women that reminded him of his own dead mother. Before Gein's grotesque fetishes were tragically unearthed, the townsfolk of Plainfield considered him a harmless—albeit slightly odd—local character. He would often babysit area youth and even took about to bringing his neighbors what he called a "venison stew" for them to enjoy. One of Gein's former neighbors told me that he vividly recalled being a young kid at the time when Gein brought over one of his homemade delicacies as a gift. With a grimaced face, the former neighbor told me that his mother had noticed the stew had peculiar smell to it and thankfully quickly tossed it out.

One of the most infamous photos of Ed Gein

Psychologists routinely debate the role of nature vs. nurture when trying to dissect the inner workings of human personality. Born in La Crosse, Wisconsin, in 1906, Edward Theodore Gein would have been a perfect argument for those advocating for nurture. Throughout his life Gein would cling to an unusually close relationship with his religiously domineering and women-hating mother. Rumors of their relationship being incestuous have never been substantiated. Even so, Gein's mother held a powerful grip over her easily influenced son.

Due to an onslaught of media reports, Hollywood movies, and shock-based websites, Gein's legacy has been boiled down that of a maniacal serial killer. Yet contrary to this popular belief, only two murders have been attributed to him. Reportedly, the first time Gein took a human life occurred in 1954 when he shot and killed a local bar owner named Mary Hogan. Three years later, Gein would strike again, and this time his sloppiness would lead to the discovery of Plainfield's real life monster. On February 16, 1957, Bernice Worden, a 58-year-old hardware store owner, suddenly went missing. When her son, who happened to be a sheriff deputy, returned from a hunting trip, he walked into the store to find his mother missing, blood splashed on the floor, and the cash register gone. Looking over the store for clues, the son found the last receipt of sale was for a jug of antifreeze and he immediately thought of Gein, who just one day earlier had come into the store asking about antifreeze. There was no way officers who headed out to Gein's house could have prepared themselves for the horror they were about to encounter.

An investigator inside of Ed Gein's old dilapidated farmhouse

The *Stevens Point Journal* described the dreadfulness of Gein's place in full detail. "You step through the kitchen door and there is an ordinary kitchen chair, except that its seat is upholstered with human skin. There is what appears to be a small bowl on the table, but it is not a bowl, it is the top half of a human skull." Townsfolk had always considered Gein a little off, always in a harmless way, but what investigators found next would forever change our perception of him. The *Stevens Point Journal* went deeper in their description of his living quarters. "Officers who went to the house found the eviscerated corpse hanging from its heels in a summer kitchen," as though it was nothing more than a gutted animal carcass. Each new step through the death house revealed terrifying new nightmares of sight. Boxes of human remains lined the floor, a belt made with human nipples was found near a pile of medical books on anatomy and embalming, and spare body parts fashioned the old farmhouse. By far, the most disturbing find was that of the rolls of human skin that had been perfectly cut and sewn together to make a full outfit that completely covered Gein's entire face and body. Later details would arise that Gein would often wear this human-skinned costume as he danced under the moonlight in his front yard. Getting an accurate tally of just how many bodies had been dug up and desecrated proved a tough task for investigators, because Gein would often only steal certain parts from each victim . . . leaving the researchers with a giant human body parts jigsaw puzzle. When all of the bowls made from human skulls, female sex organs shoved into a box, lips hanging from the shades, sawed off heads, and various other furnishings made from human skin were sorted, investigators believed that they were dealing with the stolen remains of at least a dozen different victims. Gein himself offered little explanation as to the motivation of his horrendous crimes. When questioned about the murders, he claimed that he was in a daze-like trance during the murders and body snatching and remembered little of what he had done. Psychologists opined that Gein may have been suffering from a strange sex complex (Gender Identity Disorder) that propelled him with the desire to become a woman. The *Chicago Tribune* carried the remarks of an unnamed therapist who wrote, "Gein had been extremely close to his mother throughout his life. So close in fact, that he apparently acquired a feminine complex."

With no headstone to steal, visitors often take some dirt from Gein's gravesite

Understandably, once captured Gein was found mentally unfit to stand trial and instead was sent to the State Hospital for the Criminally Insane; he later transferred to the Mendota State Hospital in Madison, Wisconsin. In 1968, Gein had miraculously improved enough to be able to stand trial for his crimes. Not surprisingly he was found guilty, yet his continued disturbed metal condition necessitated that he serve the rest of his life in a mental institution, so he was shipped back to Mendota. On July 26, 1984, Gein died of respiratory failure inside Mendota; he was 77 years old. I spoke with a retired nurse who had worked there for many years. She told me that the staff often planned social events for the residents to help with their rehabilitation. One evening a big dance was happening, and for some baffling reason, Gein found himself without a dance partner. In situations like these, the staff members were encouraged to interact with the patients, so the nurse was volunteered to be his lucky dance partner. She told me that even though Gein was extremely quiet and at that point in his life had been deemed mostly harmless, when she looked into his eyes she could still see that something was not quite right with him.

As soon as Gein's crimes were broadcast throughout newspapers around the world, hoards of curious sight seekers descended upon Plainfield looking to catch a glimpse of where the butcher of Wisconsin performed his dastardly deeds. Opportunistic businessmen looked to purchase the Gein farmhouse and open it as a gory tourist attraction, but the people of Plainfield—desperate to rid themselves of Gein's crimes—were horrified by the plans. Luckily for the town, the house "mysteriously" caught fire and burned to the ground. Even today, some 55 years later, Plainfield residents shun away from all unwanted attention that the Gein fascination brings. However, the crimes he committed were so heinous that many believe it left an indelible psychic mark on the town that can never be erased. In turn, the town of Plainfield is said to be cursed with three haunted locations that are forever tied to Ed Gein.

1. The Gein farmland where Ed lived

My first trip to Gein's old farmland turned out to be an unusual experience. Even if you are like me and have absolutely no psychic ability, the place radiates creepiness as though the land itself cannot shake the memory of past events. Just knowing what various wicked acts were conducted there is enough to make the most hardened legend tripper shudder. The place becomes infinitely more bizarre when you factor in numerous reports of visitors hearing the painful sounding cries coming from an unknown female. The horrifying cries are thought to originate from the spirit of one of the women whose body Gein desecrated.

Plenty of paranormal activity is reported on Gein's property

On my second investigation into the old Gein farmstead, I brought with me two psychics/intuitives who I had purposely kept in the dark about where we were going in order to prevent them from doing any research prior to our investigation. As far as the psychics knew, we had just pulled into another run-of-the-mill farm field. But as soon as I parked the car, my ruse was over, and the psychics immediately picked up an overwhelming amount of negative energy coupled with an intense sense of dread that caused them to refuse to exit my car. Using psychics as a research tool on an investigation can be a tricky proposition, because they often offer a mixed bag of information. Sometimes I am completely amazed by the amount of detailed information they have been able to give me without so much as ever hearing of the case before. Conversely, I have had other times where the information provided by a psychic was so far off base that I would have been better off consulting a piece of toast. Of course, using psychics is nowhere near scientific… yet I tend to include them on an investigation because so much of the knowledge of the paranormal is speculation, one never knows what might just work. I have always held the belief that when you are dealing with the strange, what is too strange?

Worden's hardware store at the time of the murder

2. The hardware store where Mrs. Worden was murdered

Former workers reported all kinds of unexplainable things taking place inside the store. Common occurrences included store items disappearing only to be found in unusual places, odd noises that could not be identified, and a general sense that one was not alone while inside the building. One former hardware employee I spoke with reported being witness to several strange events while working at the store. On one occasion while he was busy stocking the shelves, he noticed what appeared to be a woman standing at the back of the store. Believing that the woman was a customer that had quietly entered the building without him noticing, the man went over to offer his assistance, only to see the woman disappear into thin air. The employee was convinced that the paranormal activity was directly related to the 1957 murder.

One of the cemeteries where Gein dug up his victims

3. The cemetery where Gein dug up some of his victims

Visitors to this cemetery may be disappointed to find that Ed Gein currently has no gravestone marking his grave. Since he died, a morbid game of cat and mouse would occur when unhinged visitors looking to take a piece of Gein with them would steal his gravestone, only to return it after experiencing a string of bad luck and misfortune. After several thefts, the authorities finally just removed the stone to prevent any future thefts. It is now common practice for visitors to snatch a handful of dirt from his gravesite to keep as a gruesome souvenir. Outside of the grave dirt, many people leave the cemetery with the belief that it is haunted by the tormented souls whose eternal rest was forever shattered. Reports of mysterious balls of light hovering through the cemetery are very common, as are those who capture strange orbs on their photos. The overriding feel of the cemetery is that when you enter, you are not alone. One can almost picture Gein out at the cemetery at night digging up the bodies of women he was fascinated by, which may account for the ghostly sightings of an odd looking man crouched down over cemetery graves. Those who have seen this ghost leave convinced that Ed Gein still continues to torment the people of Plainfield, even though he had been dead for over 25 years.

Babyland Cemetery

Location:

Evergreen Cemetery
3415 E Hill Rd.
Grand Blanc, MI 48439
(810) 694–6541

Haunting:

At first glance nothing looks out of the ordinary at the Evergreen Cemetery. Like most cemeteries, Evergreen is neatly kept and stocked full of grave markers, flowers, and family memories. Yet if you deepen your investigation, you will see that this "ordinary" cemetery is also home to bizarre shadows, disembodied lights, and chanting robed figures. What makes this cemetery stand out from other run-of-the-mill graveyards is the unique section of graves called "Babyland." This area is filled with the graves of infants and young children who met death at an early age. In a testament to the sadness of the place, loved ones routinely leave toys and assorted stuffed animals to decorate the graves. It doesn't take long for Babyland's tales of misery, misfortune, death, and dismemberment, to uncomfortable settle in around you. Just reading the painful stories on the gravestones is more than enough to send sentimental visitors heading for the exits.

Offerings are often left at the graves of the infants

Being that the concept of Babyland is so strange, it comes as no surprise that rumors of paranormal activity abound. One evening the cemetery superintendent spotted some weird lights flickering next to a far off grave. As he started walking toward the odd lights, he noticed that they were coming from a group of robed figures huddled together holding candles.

The worker swore that he could hear chanting, and it looked like the group was performing some type of bizarre ritual. The man quietly crept closer trying to avoid detection, but as soon as the robed figures caught sight of him they disappeared into the darkness. Over the years, many different staff members have heard unexplained sounds coming from inside the cemetery. The most commonly reported noise is that of phantom footsteps that can be heard moving throughout the cemetery. Intrigued by the mystery, staff members will often try to track the mysterious footsteps until they suddenly stop, leading the staff to believe that whoever was making them knew they were being followed.

Dark shadows are often seen moving throughout the cemetery

I spoke with a long time employee who, over the years, had personally witnessed several unexplained events inside the cemetery. While sitting at her desk working she would often hear the inside chimes ring as though someone had just opened the front door, yet much to her surprise, every time she looked up, no one was standing there, and the door was completely closed. The woman also reported that on many occasions she had spotted strange, dark shadows moving around the building and the cemetery. She believed that in addition to the cemetery, the main office was haunted by the spirit of the young children as well. For years reports of these mysterious shadows have been plaguing the cemetery. Day workers often spot these unknown shadows floating throughout the cemetery. All attempts to track these shadows have failed, leaving many to believe that they are under some type of intelligent control.

As you can imagine, the peculiar nature of having a section designated solely for infants tends to attract a wide variety of curious folks. Several different ghost hunting groups have set up investigations in the cemetery to try and explain the mystery. Usually groups discover strange mists and unexplained orbs on their photos. Psychics who visit the location claim to pick up the presence of countless spirits from those who died at such a young age. If you find yourself in Babyland, you may want to bring a present to avoid being cursed by those who make their eternal home inside the cemetery.

Terror Bridge

Tara, Iowa

Terror Bridge

Location:

Tara Bridge—220th Street
Tara, Iowa (Now just outside of Fort Dodge)

Haunting:

Way out in the middle of nowhere, in a former town that has been all but forgotten, there is an old rusted train bridge where history isn't the only thing that refuses to die. The former town of Tara dates backs to 1892, but today—as the city of Fort Dodge encroaches—Tara mainly exists in the memory of those who are still sprinkled throughout the rural area. At the heart of Tara is the old railroad bridge that functioned as a life line to former residents who relied on the railway for commerce, supplies, and transportation. It seems only fitting that as the town has slowly disappeared in recent times, it is once again the train bridge that keeps Tara's memory alive. But perhaps "alive" isn't the most accurate description... the area is home to a mysterious disembodied light, the spirit of a murderous woman, and a wild dog-like creature that many people believe to be a werewolf.

Historically, the area around the bridge has always been looked at with some trepidation from those who knew it well. Before becoming known as "Terror Bridge," the area was frequently called Hinton Hollow and Deadman's Hollow—the latter being a fitting name for a place whose haunted reputation dates back to the 1800s. According to *Douglas Township Historical Story* edited by Bernice Hicks and Ruby Woodbury, several farmhands were out in the fields haying when a ferocious wind kicked in, making it nearly impossible to continue working. One of the more brazen of the men cursed the wind in hopes that it would die down and they could return to haying. Apparently the curse was not appreciated, because no sooner than the curse was spoken, the man dropped dead on the spot. Shortly after this incident, residents began reporting being chased through the area by a mysterious, howling ghost rider.

In 1891, a young railroad employee named William Roberts was working on the bridge with a pile driving crew when a flying pile ended his life. A few years after his death, bizarre events began to take place at the bridge. According to an article in the *Burlington Hawk-Eye* dated June 8, 1893, railroad men were convinced that the bridge was haunted after they witnessed several unexplainable and eerie events. The first sighting happened when the patrolling station agent spotted "the headlight of a locomotive" on the bridge. Thinking that a careless agent in Des Moines had failed to notify him of an approaching special train, the man "rushed back to his instrument and wired Des Moines, asking about the special,"—only to be told there was no such train. Mystified by the sighting, the agent decided to investigate and walked down to the train trestle where he discovered that the light was no longer there. Convinced that he had not simply imagined the light, the man was quite baffled by its sudden disappearance and quickly made his way back to the station.

GHOST OF A PILE DRIVER.

A Small Wooden Bridge Near Tara Said
by Railway men to be Haunted—
Other News.

A 1891 newspaper article describing the ghostly activity of Terror Bridge

A few evenings after the first sighting, the odd lights made another strange appearance. This time it was witnessed by a Section Foreman named Chelgren, whose story was covered in the *Eldora Ledger* on June 8, 1893. The paper tells of the bizarre event, writing that Chelgren was "returning after nightfall with his station men pumping away cheerfully on a hand car and figuring on getting their belated suppers just as soon as possible. As they neared the North Lizard bridge all the men noticed the light of a locomotive, apparently moving on the bridge. They stopped the hand car with a jerk and hustled the car off the track to let the train pass. The light came no nearer and, after waiting awhile, they put the car back on the rails and slowly pumped up to the bridge. As they approached it, the light grew dimmer and dimmer and totally disappeared. There was no sight or sound of a train. A superstitious fear came over the crowd of men and they did not have the courage to cross the bridge. They waited, talking to each other in awe-struck whispers. Suddenly, strange sounds floated on the night air with startling distinctness. The listeners heard the clanking and rattling of machinery and then a dull thud, like the falling of a pile driver. Then again came silence. The men were badly rattled and were afraid to cross the bridge. Finally, they took the hand car down the track and, giving it a good start, sent it rolling over the bridge without any occupants." The article continues that since so many skeptical citizens had reportedly seen the ghost light and heard the phantom sounds of the pile driver that the town was in a "ferment of excitement" over the whole affair. Apparently, the supernatural fervor was so high that for the next several nights ghost hunting parties trekked out to the bridge in search of the spirits, but none had been able to "capture his ghostship."

Be sure to secure your doors and windows while driving on the bridge

Sometime, years ago, another more gruesome legend of the bridge began to surface. This story told of a distraught mother who found that life with her small children was too chaotic… the constant stress eventually pushed her into a full mental breakdown. Without the ability to think clearly the mother believed that the old bridge provided her an opportunity to escape the demanding responsibilities of her life. The woman gathered up her kids and drove out to the bridge, parked her car, and waited for the next train to pass by and relieve her of her pain. When she heard the sounds of the train rumbling down the line, the woman readied her children. As soon as the train was near, she tossed her kids off the bridge onto the rushing train. With her children disposed of, the woman followed suit and leapt to her death below. The murder/suicide was said to have left a psychic scar on the bridge that still can be felt today. Many visitors to the bridge report that on quiet nights they have heard the eerie screams from the deceased children who are forced to spend eternity roaming the site where they perished. A female spirit (presumably that of the mother) had also been spotted roaming the area of the bridge. The dare tells that if you visit the bridge at night and do not lock your car windows and doors, the angry spirit of the mother will try to throw you off the bridge. Several legend trippers have also reported having mechanical issues with their vehicles at the bridge. Common problems seem to be dead batteries, cars abruptly shutting down on the bridge, and vehicles that refuse to start. Since my initial visit and investigation into the bridge back in 2006, I have been scouring through old newspapers trying to locate any article detailing the murder/suicide of a mother and her children. As of today, I have been unable to find any supporting evidence of the heart-breaking crime.

A werewolf looking creature prowls the area surrounding the bridge

If the ghostly appearance of a crazed, murdering, and suicidal mother is not quite enough incentive to visit the bridge, the stories are about to become much more bizarre. During my research to the area, I dug up a strange report from Ray Flaherty's book *Our Lizard Creek Farm* which discussed a rumor sometime ago that claimed "there was a wild man living in our woods, seeking shelter from the rains either underneath the trees or under the railroad bridge." Although seen by several residents, not all who saw the "wildman" were convinced that it was indeed a man. An article by Deann Haden Luke reported that one day a mother, her son, and a friend were driving along near Tara when they spotted an unknown animal of enormous size run right past their car at a high rate of speed. They were able to gather a good look at the creature, and what surprised them most was that—whatever it was—it appeared to be a biped, running upright on its hind legs. Since the initial sighting of the beast, others have also witnessed what is thought to be the very same creature... a creature the size of a giant bear with thick matted down fur covering its body, a long projecting snout, and the ability to effortlessly run on its hind legs. The most common creature description I get from witnesses is that of a "werewolf."

Nearly 125 years have now passed since the original ghost reports were heavily covered by the local newspapers, and in all that time we are no closer to explaining away the bizarre events than the ghost hunters were back in 1893. Maybe the strange occurrences of Terror Bridge will never be explained... but perhaps that is what makes this case so alluring.

Death Curve

Location:

A fence post located near a large tree marks the corner.
Timber Ridge Road (950 N)
Cambridge, IL

Haunting:

"Don't go out to Death Curve at night by yourself!" That was the warning given to me by nearly everyone I spoke with about the infamous local legend. It was during the summer of 2006 that I first made my way to the outskirts of Cambridge, IL, in search of the real history of a rural legend the locals referred to as "Death Curve." For decades, the legend of an ax-wielding female ghost haunting the road leading to her former farmhouse has been passed down from generation to generation. With such a long history of being told and re-told, it is easy to see why there are many versions of this legend. After repeated visits to the local courthouse, library, cemetery, and historical society, I was able to dig up the woman's death certificate, several original newspaper articles on the case, and numerous first-hand accounts of those who have survived Death Curve. Unfortunately, I also discovered that sometimes the truth can shine a terrible light into the gruesome and evil side of human nature.

At approximately 11am on the morning of September 30, 1905, thirty-one-year-old mother of seven Julie Markham sent her two oldest children off to fetch some water so they would not be privy to the horrors that she was about to commit. With the two oldest (and strongest) kids off on chores, Julie grabbed the family wood cutting ax. Then, according to the *Janesville Daily Gazette*, Julie "called the children into the house one at a time and cut their throats with the ax." With her five youngest children disposed off, Julie waited for the remaining two children to return from the well. A few moments later, when the two oldest children retuned with the water, she continued her frenzied rampage by taking the ax to them as well, completely crushing the skull of her oldest son. In the span of just a few minutes, Julie had violently taken the life of all seven of her young children. Once all of the children had met their fate by the hands of the ax, Julie calmly grabbed a butcher knife from the kitchen and tried to end her own life by gouging at her throat. However, luck was not on her side, as the knife she had grabbed was a bit dull, and the wound did not immediately kill her. Finally grasping what she had done, Julie quickly rounded up the bloodied lifeless bodies of her chopped up children and laid them side by side in the family bed. Realizing that her neck wound would not be fatal, Julie gathered up some coal oil and doused her children with it, and struck a match. Soon the whole house was ablaze, triggering the aid of observant neighbors who rushed to the scene just in time to see the horrific evidence of the murders. According to the October 5th edition of the *Cambridge Chronicle*, Julie remained in the burning house until "practically all her clothing was burned off" before stumbling outside. A doctor was quickly called to the fire, along with the sheriff and his deputy. Amazingly, by the time the doctor arrived, Julie was still alive and kicking. The doctor, not knowing the full details of the case, tried to stop the bleeding from her neck with a few stitches. The *Adams County Free Press* reported that Julie initially denied any responsibility for the murders and fire, instead claiming that the "crime had been committed by a strange man." But later, after hearing the doctor's news that her condition was fatal, she finally confessed, telling the Sheriff exactly how she had gone about the reprehensible deed. The *Cambridge Chronicle* claimed that Julie's actions were so ghastly that it registered as one of the "the most dastardly deeds that has ever occurred in Henry County." At three o'clock in the afternoon, Julie finally succumbed to her injuries and joined her children in death. The *Cambridge Chronicle* wrote, "The suffering of the woman from the self-inflicted knife wound and severe burns were something dreadful."

A newspaper article breaks the gruesome news of the murders

The father and husband, Clarence Markham, who in many versions of the legend had previously died of some unknown illness, was working at a nearby farm and was told of the events and rushed home to the unspeakable awfulness. By then the home was completely burned to the ground, and the "bodies of the seven children were found side by side in a pile of ashes in one corner of the house, burned and charred so they were unrecognizable. All the children, with some difficulty, were finally discovered, their limbs and arms being burned off." Strangely, the *Cambridge Chronicle* claimed that Julie "seemed perfectly sane after the deed had been committed," and it turns out that this was not the first time Julie had snapped. The *Cambridge*

Chronicle reported that Mrs. Markham had a history of suicidal behavior, and had, ten years prior, tried to take her own life by throwing herself into a well. Her attempt at suicide failed when she was "saved" by rescuers who believed she had accidentally fallen into the well. Friends and family who knew Julie before her marriage to Mr. Markham believed that she was not of sound mind. It seemed like they might be right, when later that day a mail carrier on his route found a letter in a nearby mailbox that was addressed to Mr. Markham. The letter provided proof that the murders were premeditated and not simply an act of rage or a temporary bout of insanity. The letter, published by the *Cambridge Chronicle*, was from Julie to her husband and read:

> Dear Clarence: This is to say goodbye to you. Some give their souls for others, and I will do this for my children. God bless them! They will all die happy in the arms of Jesus. I will meet them there, and some day you will join us too.

Believe it or not, the case took an even more tragic turn when later that same evening the father, dreadfully distraught over the loss of his entire family, decided that life was no longer worth living, and he too joined his family in death. The *Soda Springs Chieftain* reported on the suicide, writing that Mr. Markham "committed suicide by shooting himself after tying a rope around his neck so that it would choke him to death in case the bullet failed to do its purpose." Due to the lack of finances, all seven children could not be buried separately, so Mrs. Markham was buried in one grave, while what was left of her seven charred children was dumped into another grave. Both unmarked graves can still be found right down the road at Rosedale Cemetery.

Unfortunately, nothing of the Markham farmhouse where the murders took place remains today. In front of where the old farmhouse once stood is the infamous "Death Curve" where the ghost of Julie Markham is said to haunt. Over the years the road has been home to numerous car accidents, and rather than blame the sharp left turn in the otherwise straight road, the blame gets placed squarely on the ghost of Julie. The legend tells of unsuspecting motorists, unaware of the area's sorted past, being forced off the road by the appearance of an ax-carrying woman covered in blood. The legend has been brewing for decades, as I spoke with several residents that recalled stories from their childhood where they were warned about Death Curve. A lot of the mysterious paranormal activity seems to surround the old fence post that is positioned on the side of Death Curve. I interviewed a local woman who vividly remembered a bizarre event that happened to her back when she was in high school. The year was 1988, and after hearing so many stories of the area, she finally garnered up enough courage to visit Death Curve, the place that all of her friends were talking about. While most of her friends set off through the cornfields searching the land for the ghost of Julie, she decided that she would stay back in the car and take things at her own pace. She was nervously watching the fields for the return of her friends when suddenly something white floated off the fence post and moved into the cornfield before disappearing into the darkness. Another woman I spoke with had also visited the site and came away with a similar experience. She, too, was out at the curve exploring the area when a small unidentified light began to dance around the land. Bobbing up and down, the light seemed to have no distinct shape or form. Terrified by the strange light, the woman did not stick around long enough to find out what it was.

Old fencepost where a mysterious light has been spotted

Needless to say, with such a gruesome history—coupled with a remote location—Death Curve is a popular place to visit for those looking to have a paranormal experience. In addition to the mysterious balls of light, many curious visitors have seen the ghostly images of young children playing near Death Curve. Based on the description of their clothing and fashion style, the spirits are believed to be that of the murdered Markham children. These young spirits have also been seen moving throughout Rosedale Cemetery, where their unmarked grave holds what was left of their remains. Is it possible that the events of September 30, 1905 were so brutally horrific that it condemned the murdered children to eternally roam the place where their love for their mother, along with their heads, were forever severed? And what would become of Julie? Perhaps her spirit is trapped at Death Curve in order to find forgiveness for the unconscionable crimes she committed against her family? Or is her spirit still locked in a bout of craziness looking to use her ax on any passing visitor? Even more interesting is the fact that no sightings of the father's ghost have been spotted. I guess that his eagerness to join his family in death did not carry over into the afterlife.

Farmland now covers the area where the farm house once stood

In February of 2011, I returned to Cambridge on a legend trip with noted paranormal researchers Kevin Nelson and Noah Voss. Our goal was to re-visit the site where the old farmhouse once stood in an effort to encounter Julie's spirit and possibly find the answers to the abovementioned questions. Heading out of town from Cambridge, we had just about reached our destination when our vehicle suddenly lurched off the road and crashed into the snow packed ditch. Our hopes that Julie had shown up and somehow pushed our car off the road were dashed, as we ultimately blamed the accident of Kevin's poor driving. After a few minutes of shoveling ourselves out, we were back on the road and back at Death Curve. Digging through our heaping pile of research equipment, I grabbed a hatchet and placed it on the fence post hoping that it would entice the spirit of Julie into action (hopefully non-deadly action). Often times during investigations we will try to recreate things that might be familiar to the deceased spirit in order to help them spring into action. For example, if the spirit of a young child loved trains while alive, we will bring in a toy train, hoping to spark some activity. Since Julie's last memories of this life would have been tied to that bloody ax, it seemed a fitting, albeit dangerous, attempt at luring her out—one in which she did not respond to. With banks of deep, heavy snow covering the ground, we were not in a position to further explore the land where the farmhouse burned to the ground. Although nothing out of the ordinary occurred during our investigation, we could not deny that the grisly history of the area seemed to cast a dark shadow on the land that continues to this day. We left the area with the hope that someday in death Julie might be able to find the peace of mind that eluded her in life.

Mary's Murder

Elk Creek, Wisconsin

Mary's Murder

Location:

Elk Lake Dam
Elk Creek, WI

Haunting:

During the late 1990s, I received a phone call that would initiate one of the most active and intriguing paranormal cases I have ever investigated. It all began one evening when two friends were hanging out at the secluded Elk Lake Dam. Sitting on the rocky banks that run parallel to the water, the men were taking in the tranquil cascade of the water as it flowed by. Sensing that something wasn't right, one of the friends looked back over his shoulder and saw a "glowing woman in white" standing back a few feet from him.

He immediately nudged his buddy and asked, "Do you know there is a glowing woman in white standing next to us?" His buddy grimly said, "Yes, but I don't want to turn around and look." After a tense few minutes, the friends found the collective courage to spin around, only to discover that the woman was gone. The two men wasted little time hightailing it out of the area. A few days later, one of the friends had calmed down enough to report the incident. In our phone conversation it was made clear that the other witness had sworn never to go back to Elk Lake Dam again. With a little persuading I was able to get the caller to reluctantly return to the dam to show us exactly where the glowing woman had appeared.

Strange mist appearing at the dam

During this time period I was a college student studying psychology at the University of WI-Stout, and one of my cohorts, a fellow named Aaron, believed that he was psychic and could pick up the spirits of those who have passed away. I decided to ask Aaron to come along on this case. If the place was haunted, perhaps Aaron would be able to pick up on something that the rest of us non-psychic researchers could not. Together with the original witness, Aaron and I traveled out to the dam in search of the mysterious glowing woman. Located only ten miles outside of the city of Eau Claire,

Wisconsin, the Elk Lake Dam area feels as if it is a thousand miles from safety. The aging dam site appears as if it is straight out of a horror movie. If anyplace looks like it should be haunted, it is the Elk Lake Dam. The dam site sits on the edge of Elk Creek Lake, and it is surrounded by thick, eerie-looking woods that appear to close in around you. We soon discovered that the only way to reach the location of the ghost sighting is by hiking down the rocky hill through the thick woods to reach the water. Once you escape from the woods, the crashing of the cascading water drowns out any outside noise. A general sense of claustrophobia squeezes visitors as they soon realize that the only means of escape is by diving into the water or by blindly running back uphill through the woods. Trying to shake the discomforting aura of the place, Aaron and I begin to snap a few photos of the area where the witnesses spotted the young woman. Keep in mind that this was prior to the advent of digital photos, so all we could do was wait and see what the pictures revealed when they were developed. For one of the photos, Aaron and I stood on opposite ends of where the woman had been spotted and simultaneously tried to take a photo of the spot. The only problem was that Aaron's camera would not work. It had been working fine just seconds before, and would work perfectly through the rest of the investigation, yet at the moment of our duel picture taking his camera simply would not take the picture. We recorded the camera malfunction in our journal and made a note to later check my version of the photo as my camera worked just fine. After a few hours of exploring the area, taking photos, recording for any EVPs (electronic voice phenomenon), and further interviewing the witness, we decided to call it a night. Although nothing overtly paranormal occurred during our first visit, the place emitted such a weird vibe that we held out hope that our equipment might offer up some evidence.

Mysterious white mist captured at the dam

The next day we had our film developed, and were surprised to discover that one of the photos I had taken showed a mysterious white fog-like substance in the upper right corner. Obviously, when we took the photos, no type of anomaly was noted with our naked eye, but what really struck us as the most bizarre, was the fact that in the background of the photo you can clearly see Aaron fidgeting with his problematic camera. It turns out the picture with the unexplained substance in it was the one that was taken at the exact moment when Aaron's camera mysteriously failed to work. Bolstered by the odd photo, I decided to venture back to the dam with a few other investigators. When we reached the seclusion of the dam, a couple of investigators decided to remain on the bridge, while the rest of us headed straight down to the water. No more than ten minutes had passed when suddenly a strange scream pierced the night air. The baffling shriek sounded as though it was part female, and part mechanical noise. Whatever it was, it didn't sound like anything I had heard before, so quickly I radioed up to the investigators on the bridge to see what they made of the scream, only to find out that no noise was heard from the bridge. The only thing we could think of was that the odd noise perhaps came from a passing car radio. Our theory was quickly shot down when we learned that no cars had passed by while we were down at the water. Even more bizarre was the fact that the mysterious noise was not picked up on any of our audio or video recorders.

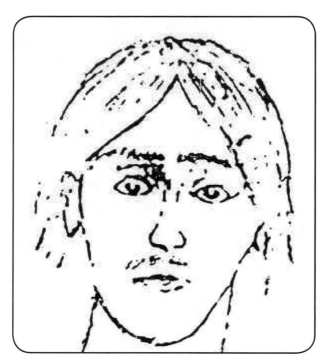

Witness description of Mary's killer

At this point in time, I began getting so many stories of odd things happening at the dam that I started to talk about the case at many of my lectures. After one such lecture, a gentleman approached me and told me that he had lived out in the general area of the dam during the 1970s, and vaguely remembered a brutal murder that took place near his home, but he had no further details. Believe it or not, the seemingly limited information that he could provide about the incident was much more than I normally receive. At least this story had a decade attached to it, unlike most stories that I receive that only allude to an event taking place sometime in the last hundred years or so. With this new break in the case, I began searching through the 1970s edition of the local newspaper, looking for reports of a murder in the area. Then, as I was making my way through 1974, I discovered the horrific murder that the gentleman told me about. On the fateful morning of February 15, Mary Schlais, a bright and attractive twenty-five-year-old woman from Minneapolis, was thought to be hitchhiking her way down to Chicago. Later that afternoon, the Sheriff's department received a concerned call from a local Elk Lake resident, who upon returning to his home in the area, had spotted someone who seemed to be suspiciously kicking snow and leaves over something large near the trunk of a small gold colored car that was parked on the side of the road. Sensing that something wasn't quite right, the resident called the Sheriff's Department. Investigators quickly arrived at the crime scene and noticed that the unknown object the man was kicking snow over was in fact the dead, blood soaked body of young Mary. Investigators began collecting evidence, and determined that Mary had been viciously stabbed over a dozen times, including several deep defensive cuts to her hands and arms. With the exception of Mary's bloody body, investigators had little other evidence to go on. A stocking cap found at the scene provided no DNA or hair samples, and tire impressions found on the road (presumably from the gold car) gave little help to the search. The witness was able to provide a basic description of the mysterious man, and the authorities did release a general sketch of the alleged murderer, but that too failed to generate any serious leads. Local gossip pointed the finger at several suspects, including the man who first notified the police, but no charges were ever filed against anyone, and over the years the case grew cold, finally forcing officers to put it on the shelf.

Mary Schlais

Now, armed with the new information, I decided to conduct another investigation at the dam. If the place was truly haunted, maybe it was haunted by the spirit of young Mary. With me again this time was Aaron (the psychic) who requested that we take a couple photos of the old cement pillar near the water. When the photos came back, one of them showed another strange mist floating in the air. After a few more hours we were finishing up the investigation and were about to head back home when Aaron got the uneasy feeling that Mary had followed us back to our vehicles, and was now standing right behind us. We snapped one last photo for the evening, a photo that many believe captured evidence of Mary's spirit haunting the old dam.

Evidence of Mary's ghost?

Over the years, hundreds of curious legend trippers have ventured out to the dam in search of Mary's spirit. I could easily write an entire book on the strange happenings of the area, but for the sake of leaving space for other gruesome cases, I will include only a few of my favorite occurrences. One day I received a call from a guy asking how the woman of Elk Lake Dam had died. The reason for his curiosity arose from a recent trip he and a friend had taken out to the dam. One night the two friends had a spur of the moment urge to go out and see the haunted dam. The two men spilt up and began exploring the eeriness of the area. A few minutes later, the man spotted his friend standing on the side of the bridge intently peering into the water below. When the man approached, he saw that he friend appeared to be in some sort of weird trance, and to make matters worse, he was attempting to climb the bridge rail and jump over the side. The man frantically ran and grabbed his friend, physically pulling him off from the edge of the bridge. Once at the safety of the center of the bridge, the confused friend seemed to snap out of his trace and began sobbing, demanding that they leave the area immediately. While driving back to town, the friend finally calmed down enough to say that while on the bridge he felt as though he was possessed by the spirit of a woman who was forcing him to commit suicide by jumping over the side. His friend had called me wondering if Mary's cause of death was suicide, thinking that it was the spirit of Mary that had possessed his friend. By the sound of his voice, he was not at all relieved when I told him that Mary's cause of death was murder, not suicide.

In 2004, a middle school student spoke to me about a strange incident that happened while he was out on Elk Lake fishing with his dad. The father and son anglers had fished through the early morning hours, and as noon was approaching they anchored their boat near the dam, hoping the area would provide some much needed luck. After several casts the boy caught sight of a floating woman out of the corner of his eye. Spinning his head, he spotted a nearly transparent "glowing woman" that seemed to be watching over him with a sinister "blank stare" that sent chills running through the young man. Shaking his head with disbelief, the woman suddenly disappeared into thin air.

In 2005, I received an email from a woman whose encounter at the dam echoed what I had experienced several years prior. One evening the brave young woman set out with her boyfriend to uncover the secrets of the dam. Neither of them had been to the dam before, so they were a bit disappointed when they arrived and found that the area did not appear "too scary." The couple sat around talking for awhile when, out of nowhere, three screams echoed in the wind. The once calming environment suddenly became "so scary" to the frightened couple. Convinced that they were alone at the bridge, the couple ruled out the possibility that someone was playing a cruel trick on them. The woman stated that the screams sounded like they came from a girl and sounded muffled, yet at the same time they were inexplicably loud. The couple gathered up there things and tore off from the area. I was immediately interested in this story as it paralleled my odd scream experience (although I had not publicly talked about the scream I had heard several years earlier).

Much like the problems we were having with our research equipment, Terry Fisk and I also had heard stories of construction workers who were also plagued by mysterious equipment difficulties. Workers told us that they would often bring in machines to work on the rundown dam, only to end up hauling them out because they would not start up at the dam. Once removed from the area, the machines would start working perfectly, but each time the equipment was brought back to the dam, it would always malfunction.

Perhaps the oddest of all events to have taken place at the dam was the incredible story of Virginia Hendricks. At a paranormal conference a woman approached Terry Fisk and me with a story so bizarre that if it was true, it might just prove that the spirit haunting Elk Lake Dam was that of Mary Schlais. Virginia lived in a home right next to the dam and reported that in the fall of 1994, she was regularly visited by a mysterious young woman. Virginia described the woman as being pretty, in her early 20s, with shoulder length blond hair. The visitor, who always dressed in a pink angora sweater and white Capri pants, would walk up through the garden and tap on Virginia's window. Virginia thought this woman was a ghost because she always showed up at the exact same time during her morning or afternoon visits. Virginia would often bring food and drink out to the woman who only identified herself as "Mary." The only problem with this tantalizing tale was that we could not ask Virginia about it, because she had died in 1995. The woman sharing the story with us was Virginia's daughter, who had listened to the bizarre stories from her mother and feared that her mom had become senile in her old age. It wasn't until she heard of our research that she began to believe that her maybe her mother wasn't losing her mind after all.

I hold a special affinity toward this legend because it is one of my longest running investigations. In 1999, I sat down and interviewed Dunn County Sheriff John Kanta, who confirmed that Mary had been stabbed repeatedly, although no sign of sexual assault was present. At this point in time the case had been nearly all but forgotten by the general public, and Kanta answered as many questions as he could without jeopardizing the ongoing cold case. The most heartening aspect of this case is that so many people have traveled to the bridge to see Mary's ghost, and so many media outlets have relentlessly covered the haunting, that it has rekindled interest into the grisly unsolved murder of Mary. In fact, in 2009, authorities exhumed Mary's body in hope of finding new DNA evidence that might lead to her killer. I knew things had changed when, in the process of writing this book, I once again contacted the Dunn County Sheriff's Department looking for any new information on Mary's death. This time I got no interview and was politely told that no information could be given since the case was now considered active. Hopefully, one day the case will be solved, thereby allowing Mary's spirit to finally rest peacefully.

Misfortune at the Fenton Hotel

Location:

302 N. Leroy St.
Fenton, MI
(810) 750- 9463
www.fentonhotel.com

Haunting:

The Historic Fenton Hotel has dutifully served the community for over 150 years. Although the business no longer offers lodging to weary travelers, the beautifully restored restaurant still provides a central gathering place where both locals and travelers feel at ease. At this place you will not have to look hard in order to find the legends, as the haunted history is listed right on the menu.

The bar room is home to many odd sightings

The property itself dates back to 1856, when the original Vermont House was constructed. Throughout the last 150 years the place has undergone a plethora of renovations, name changes, and different owners, but one thing that has survived the test of time is all of the paranormal activity that happens inside the building's walls. The owner of the place was quick to share with me one of the main legends that surrounds his historic property. Years ago a young local woman was working as a server at the hotel when she fell head over heels in love with a suave traveling salesman. A hot romance quickly brewed between the two until the woman discovered she was unexpectedly pregnant. Upon hearing the unwelcome news, the salesman firmly stated that he wanted nothing more to do with the woman and unceremoniously skipped town without delay. The young woman was beyond heartbroken and fell into a pit of depression. She became so distraught at the thought of being an unwed mother that she grabbed a rope and hanged herself from the second floor window. Now the spirit of the suicidal server is thought to be one of the main ghosts haunting the place. Her spirit is now most often seen, heard, and felt inside the women's bathroom. The owner stated that over the last few years three different people have had a weird experience with a spirit while using the third stall of the women's restroom. One customer even claimed that while she was using the facilities, she could feel someone lightly pulling at her hair. At one time during the building's long history, many rooms at the hotel were rented by women who worked as ladies of the night at nearby houses of ill repute. It is suggested that some of the female activity may be caused by one of their spirits that has refused to move on.

A mysterious woman is often seen roaming the restaurant

In her book *Weird Michigan*, researcher Linda Godfrey writes that another of the resident ghosts is that of a long-time caretaker named Emery. While alive, Emery enjoyed the comforts of his upstairs lodging. Even though he has long since passed, his footsteps can be clearly heard rattling the building's tin ceiling as he paces back and forth near his old third floor dwelling. Staff members are reminded of Emery on numerous occasions while closing up for the evening; they have heard unexplained pounding and thumping coming from the area of his old room. Workers believe that all the activity is simply his subtle way of encouraging them to hurry up and finish their duties so he can finally get some rest for the night.

Some believe that the spirits of the hotel refuse to ever check out

It appears that the restaurant is also home to a ghost that has a fondness for whiskey. On several occasions a nicely dressed man seated at a table has ordered a glass of Jack Daniels whiskey on the rocks. However, when the drink is served, the man is nowhere to be found, leading servers to question whether he was really ever there. In *Haunted Michigan*, author Gerald Hunter tells of a young woman who was going into the back storage area to grab some liquor bottles for the bar. After securing the liquor, the woman turned around to head back and was startled by the appearance of a man in a top hat and black coat staring at her from the doorway. The woman immediately knew that the man was a ghost because he appeared in black and white.

Cases like this one are my favorites to investigate because they come complete with a long and sorted history, several possible spirits haunting the place, and dozens of first-hand witnesses. After concluding my investigation, I was mildly disappointed that I did not have a personal encounter, but I did end up with a tasty meal and a little whiskey that thankfully no spirit tried to wrestle from me.

ᛏʰe Ðay ᛏʰat Music Ðied

Location:

Farm field
Intersection of 315th St. and Gull Avenue
Clear Lake, Iowa

Haunting:

Imagine a simple flip of a coin deciding whether you will live or die. That was the case for the tragic crash that is best known as "the day the music died." Fate seemed to be against the men that took off in the plane heading for their next show. Fans of the musicians take solace in the fact that the music continues to live on after the death of their idols. However, others believe that their music isn't the only thing that continues to live on.

I love cases where a traditional haunting gets mixed in with a piece of Americana. That is exactly what happened when Waylon Jennings, Buddy Holly, Ritchie Valens and the Big Bopper (along with their bands) were on

"The Winter Dance Party" tour in 1959. Unlike the spoiled rock stars of today, their tour was one long, cold Midwest road trip. Among the many difficulties was the fact that their bus kept breaking down and often times the heat was not available. Due to the poor travel conditions, several band members had caught colds and one even developed frost bite. Finally after a gig at the Surf's Ballroom, sickness had caught up to Buddy Holly. The constant mishaps and never ending cold convinced Holly that he did not want ride the old tour bus to Moorhead, Minnesota. Holly arranged to charter a plane to Fargo, North Dakota, which was the closest town they could fly to for their next gig. The plane was only equipped to hold two other passengers, forcing band members to fight for the remaining seats. Band member Waylon Jennings ended up volunteering to give his seat to the Big Bopper, and Bob Hale flipped a coin to see if Ritchie Valens or Tommy Alsup would get the last spot on the warm plane. Valens won the coin flip that would seal his fate. Before departing, Holly used the pay phone outside the Surf Ballroom to call his brother. While leaving, Holly took the opportunity to rib Jennings who had given up his seat. Buddy joked, "You're not going on that plane with me tonight?" Jennings simply said "No." He kept his teasing going and said, "Well, I hope your old bus freezes up again." Jennings looked at his friend and jokingly replied, "Well, I hope your old plane crashes." Little did the men know that both their predictions would come true that night. The three musicians took off on a small four-passenger Beechcraft Bonanza. The plane was piloted by Roger Peterson, who was an inexperienced twenty-one-year-old pilot. The men left from the Surf Ballroom in Clear Lake heading to the Mason City Airport. A storm warning for the area did not reach the pilot. At approximately 1am, the small plane crashed into the cornfield of Albert Juhl, killing everyone on board. When the plane did not arrive in Fargo, people started to worry. The next day Jerry Dwyer mounted a search party and found the plane's wreckage along a snow covered field. The bodies were removed and buried at each of the star's various home towns. However, this is only the beginning of the story. Once the ground thawed out, the farmer found several plane parts and some personal items… along with a few stray body parts. In 1998, a Buddy Holly fan from Wisconsin constructed a memorial at the site of the crash.

Farm field where the plane crashed down

Ever since the crash, the area has taken on a mystical reputation. The legend claiming that Holly's trademark glasses were discovered by a farmer who was plowing his field 20 years after the crash only enhanced the place's grisly aura. Since the 1960s, drivers have reported seeing several ghosts wandering the spot where the plane crashed down in 1959. According to the witnesses, the ghosts were thought to be those of Buddy Holly, the Big Bopper, and Ritchie Valens. Strange out of place noises also haunt the area. Local residents report hearing a thunderous roaring noise sounding like a plane crashing into the field. Of course, when they check, no crashed planes can be found. Other visitors are often treated to a much more pleasurable noise when they hear the faint sounds of music coming from the crash site. The spectral playing is usually attributed to the fallen artists.

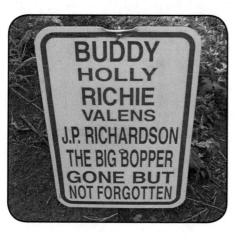

Make shift memorial to the rockers

The main reason that people believe that the farmland is haunted by Buddy Holly is because they actually see the ghost of Buddy Holly. Several people have contacted me after visiting the site to report that they caught sight of a ghostly looking image of someone resembling Buddy Holly, complete with his trademark glasses.

Unexplained music can often be heard at the memorial site

It seems that the popularity that Holly enjoyed during life has extended into the afterlife. Not only do people claim that he haunts his death site, but many have also seen his spirit haunting the nearby Surf's Ballroom, the venue that Holly played before he died.

Cry Baby Bridge
Monmouth, IL

Cry Baby Bridge

Location:

Secluded Bridge
Monmouth, IL

Haunting:

During the 1980s and 90s, the *Choose Your Own Adventure* books were enormously popular, selling over 250 million copies. The books tossed control of the story line back to the reader by allowing you to literally choose your own adventure by selecting from several different decisions that affected the outcome of the story. If you were a fan of the books, you are in luck, because the legend of Cry Baby Bridge has a smorgasbord of different stories that allow you to carefully choose your own haunted adventure. Here are just a few of the haunted stories of the bridge:

Version 1—A young couple was recklessly speeding around the curvy road when they lost control of their car, smashed over the side of the bridge, and plunged into the dark, murky river where they met their watery grave.

Version 2—A school bus full of playful children was driving round the bend and the driver lost control, sending the bus plummeting into the river. Water gushed in through the open windows while the pressure trapped the children and their lungs filled with water. When rescue crews finally got to the scene, it was too late . . . the bus was already one large submerged coffin full of dead children.

Version 3—A distraught young mother suffered a psychotic breakdown and drove out to the bridge with her young child. Exhausted from the constant battle to keep some semblance of sanity, the mother chucked her young child over the bridge where death quickly followed.

Version 4—The old bridge served as the favorite fishing hole for an elderly gentleman who frequently visited the area in hopes of catching a whopper. Old age had limited the amount of walking the man was capable of, so he usually just set up shop on the edge of the bridge. Normally, the few vehicles that did pass by slowed down and waved, some even occasionally asked how the fishing was. But one day a group of teenagers were out racing around and by the time they spotted the old man fishing from the bridge, it was too late, and the man was crushed to death under the wheels of their car.

A legend like this that contains so many stories about its origin can be quite frustrating and difficult to investigate. In my quest to sort fact from fiction, I traveled to Monmouth with hopes of finally setting the record straight. Nearly everyone I spoke with had heard haunted stories about Cry Baby Bridge. The only problem I encountered was that with each new person I talked with, I got an entirely new version of why the bridge was haunted. I spoke with reference librarians, long-time residents and local historians. I dug through old newspapers, highway records and regional books . . . yet no documented history or information about the bridge surfaced. I also came up short with finding any filed reports of accidents or deaths that occurred out at the bridge. The lone bright spot of my research came when I was able to track stories of the bridge being haunted back at least 50 years, and it is quite possible that they go back much further.

I have to say, the bridge itself is pretty creepy. Hidden out in the gravel filled back country roads, its cement foundation is covered with layers of dirt, giving the impression that the gravel road continues right across the bridge. The graffiti covering the steel trusses bears evidence of years of visitation from curious legend trippers. I am not sure if it is the secluded location, the decrepit condition of the bridge itself, or even the brown, murky water that passes underneath, but the place does give off the feel that something is not quite right.

The spirits of children will push your car to safety

But regardless of the varying stories as to why the bridge is haunted, one thing that everyone I spoke with agreed to was that the bridge was unquestionably haunted. A common narrative that weaved through the majority of the stories was that idea that the bridge was haunted by the cries of the dead children whose lives ended on the bridge and whose souls were now trapped there for eternity. I spoke with two young residents that had traveled out to the bridge one evening to see what all the fuss was about. Friends of theirs had told them that if you stop your car on the bridge and put it into neutral, the ever watchful spirits of the deceased children will push your car over the bridge safely so you do not suffer the same fate they did. Following the advice of their friends, the couple placed their car in neutral while they nervously waited. Within seconds, the couple felt their car inch forward on its own as though it was being pushed by the small hands of the dead children. Completely freaked out, the couple took control of the car and tore out of the area as fast as they could. The legend that the ghostly children will guide your car to safety was one of the more popular stories involving Cry Baby Bridge. Over the years, I have traveled to dozens of unique places where a similar phenomenon was said to take place, so I was excited to put another location to the test. Unfortunately for me, when I parked my car on the bridge the spirits of the young children refused to lend their assistance, forcing me to drive across the river the old fashioned way. After failing to entice the children to push my car, I spent the rest of my evening at the bridge with an assortment of equipment. I had packed with me several audio and video recorders, motion detectors, EMF meters, thermo scans, and some digital cameras. After several hours of research, the only thing I had to show for my efforts were some cool looking photos of the old bridge covered in moonlight.

Cries of help ring out from the bridge

The more eerie of the events to happen at the bridge come in the form of the mysterious ghastly cries that echo around the bridge. Local lore tells that the spectral cries you hear at the bridge are coming from the spirits of the dead kids who are crying out in hopes that you will help end their suffering. As I was inquiring about the bridge around town, a local woman shared the following bizarre story with me. Her adventure began late one evening when on an unexpected urge, she decided to travel out to the bridge to investigate the haunted legend. For as long as she could remember she had heard the haunted bridge stories from friends, family, and co-workers, yet over all this time, she had remained fairly skeptical. Upon arriving at the bridge she swore she could hear the faint cries of a baby coming from underneath the bridge. Thinking that her imagination was getting the better of her, she scoured the area in search of the crying sound, but was ultimately unable to locate any baby. During my investigation, I ran across another local woman who had a very similar experience to the previous one. She, too, had been out at the bridge when she heard the painful cries that sounded as though they were coming from an upset newborn. Convinced that some kids were playing a trick on her, the puzzled woman looked all over the bridge and surrounding woods, only to discover that she was the only living person out there.

The dark churning waters of the haunted river

In 2011, I traveled back to Cry Baby Bridge for a follow-up investigation. This time I brought with me noted paranormal experts Noah Voss and Kevin Nelson. The bridge is a notoriously popular stopping point for those seeking the paranormal, so we chose to visit the bridge during the heart of February, hoping that the cold temperatures and deep snow would guarantee that we would not have to worry about any unexpected visitors. We soon discovered that the main road to the bridge had not been plowed out for the winter months, forcing us to hike it through banks of deep snow just to reach the bridge. Even in the dead of the winter, when the surroundings naturally produce an eerie quiet, the bridge takes on a more creepy tone, giving off the impression that you are not supposed to be out there. After I gave the guys a quick rehash of the all the bridge stories I have been told, we shot some video, snapped some photos, and called out to the spirits of the dead children. After getting no response to our vocal bait or finding anything out of the ordinary, we decided to set off back to the safety of our far away vehicle. We had assumed that the harsh, freezing, snow ridden weather was too much, even for the non-living. Or perhaps the spirits of those dead children were just saving up their energy to push the car of the next uninitiated visitor.

Buried Alive in Sanborn
Cemetery

Lamberton, Minnesota

Buried Alive In Sanborn Cemetery

Location:

Sanborn Cemetery
100th St.
Lamberton, MN

Haunting:

For years, legends have been brewing about the mysterious goings on that take place out at the haunted Sandborn Cemetery. Perched atop of a small hill on the outskirts of town, Sandborn Cemetery is just far enough away from the city to create an eerie atmosphere, yet close enough to town to provide a modicum of security. It is at this small cemetery that people have claimed to have seen disembodied lights floating throughout the grounds. According to witnesses, these balls of light change in shape, size, and even color, as they maneuver their way about in the darkness. I spoke with a witness who was hanging out in the cemetery one evening when, out of nowhere, she spotted a strange ball of light moving about in the cemetery. Not wanting to stick around to find out what it was, the woman promptly left the grounds. One of the more commonly given solutions to any mysterious lights in a graveyard is that they are nothing more than reflections of street lamps and car headlights bouncing off of various grave markers. To test this theory while investigating the Sanborn Cemetery, I made sure to pay special attention when vehicles passed by and was unable to spot any reflecting lights. It seems that the small hill the cemetery sits on shields it from incoming headlights.

Mysterious balls of light float throughout the cemetery

The most gruesome of the cemetery legends tells the tragic tale of a young woman who many years ago had been accidently buried alive. The dare that I heard from locals was that if you ventured out to the cemetery at night, and were very quiet, you could put your ear to the ground and hear the frantic cries of the woman who had been buried alive. Witnesses claim to have heard the sounds of a female voice crying out for help from beneath the grassy earth. Reports of hearing 'help me,' 'please dig me up,' and 'I am down here,' are very common at the cemetery. With so many perplexing reports coming in from the cemetery, I was extremely excited to check out the place for myself. For my first visit I brought with me a ton of recording equipment. If the cemetery was haunted by the spectral cries of this buried alive female, I was quite certain that I would be able pick them up on tape. As it turns out, while I was there, the woman decided to clam up and remain silent. Not all was lost on the investigation though, as I did speak with a young man who told me that one evening while he was out walking through the cemetery he heard what sounded like loud female screams coming from somewhere inside the cemetery. After thoroughly searching the cemetery, the man found no visible cause for the mysterious screams and left the cemetery baffled by the unknown screams. I also spoke with an employee of a local gas station who stated that the cemetery had always given her the creeps, and when she finally garnered up the courage to visit, she swore she heard the sounds of a little girl cheerfully playing in the cemetery, but she too could not find a source for the unknown noise. Talking with several other locals, I found out that on certain nights when the wind was just right, these odd cemetery cries would be carried all the way into town. Perhaps distorted from the wind and distance, when heard in town, the cries seemed to be coming from a young infant.

Female cries of help can be heard throughout the cemetery

Over the years, I have ventured back to the cemetery several times, and each time I leave the place with no first-hand experience. The question of a woman being buried inside the cemetery still remained unanswered. After laboriously scouring through old newspaper after newspaper, I was unable to find any reports containing fears that someone had been buried alive in Sandborn Cemetery. If someone had been buried alive, it was not known (or reported) by their loved ones, which was all too common during the 1800s. The mere thought of being buried alive, helplessly trapped inside a small confining box, fighting for limited air as pure darkness engulfs you is frightening enough to make anyone shudder. Yet, many skeptics claim that the whole idea of people being buried alive is nothing more than a highly recited urban legend. However, this is far from the truth, as I am certain that thousands of people were once buried alive. How do I know this? Because I have thousands of old newspaper accounts from the late 1800s and early 1900s that describe fears from families who believe relatives had been buried alive. Back in the ol' days, whether someone was in a diabetic shock, or coma, doctors would often pronounce them dead, only to discover that many of them, (as reported in newspaper articles) even at their own funeral, would pop up from the 'dead' and be saved just in the nick of time. The thought seems a little silly to us today with our modern medicine and science, but our grandparents were so afraid of being buried alive that they came up with several inventions to thwart this. My favorite of these inventions was that of a cemetery bell. The cemetery bell was a bell that would sit over your grave with a rope and pole that would go down into your casket, so that if you awoke to find yourself buried alive, you could simply pull the rope and it would ring the bell, alerting the cemetery caretaker (who usually lived at the cemetery) that you had been buried alive. The only problem with this dandy little invention was that on many nights the wind would set off these bells, giving the caretaker quite a scare thinking that everyone had been buried alive. Needless to say, interest in cemetery bells faded out pretty quickly and they are all but extinct in the US . . . which is too bad since having one in Sanborn Cemetery would really help out with my investigation.

Deadly Shootout at Little Bohemia

Location:

Little Bohemia Lodge
142 Highway 51 S
Manitowish Waters, WI 54545
(715) 543–8433

Haunting:

It was the offseason of 1934, which meant that the Wisconsin Northwoods were completely dead; it wasn't packed full of winter tourists like it is today. Thanks to the Great Depression, the previous few years had been tough on hospitability providers, as evidenced by the sheer number of operations that had shuttered their doors. Owners hoped that the recent repeal of Prohibition was just the spark that travelers needed to revert back to their vacationing ways. It was with this sense of optimism that the owners of Little Bohemia Lodge greeted a group of travelers who pulled up and requested to rent out the entire lodge for the weekend—they said money was no object. In fact, the owners said that the men were throwing around money as though they had just robbed a bank. This should have been an important warning sign of things to come, but the owners were extremely excited—new business was desperately needed. However, their excitement quickly turned to fear when they noticed who walked through their front door. It was a virtual who's who of deadly gangsters including John Dillinger, Homer Van Meter and his girlfriend Mickey Conforti, George "Baby Face" Nelson and his wife Helen, Tommy Carroll and his wife Jean Delaney, John "Red" Hamilton and his girlfriend Pat Cherrington, and Pat Reilly. These gangsters were so dangerous that if the Feds could somehow capture this renegade group, they could practically throw away their most wanted list.

It didn't take the owners long to figure out who these well-dressed men were. Having been easily recognized, Dillinger assured the owners that the group merely wanted to enjoy some old fashioned R&R and promised that no trouble would come from their end. Tensions calmed down a bit as the gangsters began telling wonderful stories, buying rounds, and tipping really well. The only thing that concerned the owners was that all of the men seemed to have a large lump on the sides of their jackets. Sadly, the owners would soon find out what those lumps contained as they made the foolish mistake of smuggling out information to the FBI that Dillinger and his men were in the Northwoods. The FBI flew in to Rhinelander, WI, and made their way over to Voss' Birchwood Lodge, which sat just south of Little Bohemia. Learning that Dillinger, who was suppose to leave the lodge the next morning, was looking to leave at any moment, the Feds had no choice but to rush to Little Bohemia before Dillinger could get away. With no plan of action, the Feds arrived at the lodge just before 9pm. The night sky was pitch black, and the area was so wooded and mysterious that nearly anything seemed possible. The Feds were simply going to wait for Dillinger and his men to exit the building, where the law men would be waiting to capture or kill them. Although the agents were well equipped with tear gas, machine guns, and bulletproof vests, the nervousness in the air was almost palpable. Most of the young agents were relatively new to the force, and even more importantly, they were new to deadly shootouts. Now as they were about to face off against the most hardened of criminals, their minds swirled with doubt and fear. Unfortunately for the Feds, just after 9pm, three local men were leaving the lodge after a rambunctious night spent eating and drinking. They casually walked out and started up their car. With their radio blaring, the trio looked to head home for the night. Not knowing the identities of the men, the FBI panicked thinking it was Dillinger. Frantically, they demanded that the car halt, but the orders were drowned out by the booming radio. Not willing to let Dillinger escape, the agents opened fire and let loose a volley of lead on the car. All three men were struck by the bullets—one of them fatally. With blood oozing from their wounds, the two surviving men stumbled from the car into the nearby woods. Needless to say, after the shots rang out, all hell broke loose at Little Bohemia. Dillinger and his men quickly fired back as they rushed to the backside of the building, where they scurried out the back window and made their way to freedom. Baby Face Nelson, who was sleeping in a side cabin, let off a blast of bullets before sneaking off into the darkness of the woods. Later that night, Nelson would end up gunning down a car load of law officers in an attack that would kill FBI Special Agent Carter Baum.

Little Bohemia as it looked in 1934

The botched FBI raid resulted in three innocent civilians being shot (one killed) and several law enforcement agents getting shot (one killed), while all the gangsters got away scot free. Because the gangsters had to leave in such a hurry, numerous personal items—including their clothing, hygiene items, and weapons—were left behind. Much to the credit of Little Bohemia, they have made these items a part of today's dining experience at the lodge. Even more importantly, they left the original bullet holes in the lodge windows, where they still remain today.

While the gangsters themselves no longer frequent Little Bohemia, many believe that their spirits still wander the historic site. Others believe that the restless spirits of the two men gunned down in 1934 also continue to roam Little Bohemia. One of the most commonly reported areas of paranormal activity is inside the main lodge. When I first visited Little Bohemia back in 2002, staff members told me that there were times while working in the kitchen when things would inexplicably go missing without a trace, and they insisted that these missing items were not due to the forgetfulness of the staff. Other common events included cooks and wait staff hearing their names being called while no one was there or having someone (or something) tap them on the shoulder... only to turn around and find nothing there. Even more bizarre is when customers report seeing the ghostly appearances of a man walking around on the property. Witnesses often state that the apparition appeared to be wearing a fancy fedora hat and zoot suit, just like the fashions of the 1930s.

A perfect setting for phantom gangsters

Years ago, Little Bohemia used to rent out the cabin where Baby Face slept back in 1934 to visiting tourists. From the onset, guests started reporting strange things occurring inside the cabin. On many nights, guests would be awoken from bed by the sound of a Tommy gun blasting out their windows. The guests could hear the gunfire, see the gun smoke, and smell the gunpowder, yet every time they investigated, they found that the windows were in perfect undamaged condition. During the day, guests would often go out on a hike or bike ride, only to return to find that their room had been completely rearranged, even though nothing was ever found

missing. Eventually, the paranormal activity was causing so many hassles that the owners decided to turn the cabin into an amusement game room. Staff members informed me that guests repeatedly saw pool sticks fly across the room as thrown by some unseen force. The mysterious 1930s looking man was also regularly spotted inside the game room as well. Today the old cabin is mostly used for storage, making it a bit more difficult for the general public to spot the wandering ghost.

The window that provided an easy escape for the gangsters

Even with such a long history of haunted activity, no one is sure whether the spirit(s) is/are that of the FBI agent looking to settle the score with the gangsters, the gunned down innocent victim who is eternally seeking peace, or some unknown ghost that is just in search of some Northwoods R&R. Some contend that the mysterious ghost is that of John Dillinger himself. If true, it would seem that Dillinger is busier in death than he was in life, because roughly half a dozen places around the U.S. claim to be haunted by Public Enemy #1. One thing that everyone does agree upon, though, is that Dillinger and his gang only left Little Bohemia because they had to—an inconvenience that apparently does not pertain to the spirits haunting the lodge.

CASE # 23

Burned Orphans by the Lake

Location:

Luna Pier, MI

Haunting:

The legend told to each new generation of area teenagers states that many years ago a woman managed a summer camp for orphans. One morning, the woman went out for a long leisurely walk along the beautiful beach. While she was gone a terrible fire rushed through the camp burning all of the children to death. By the time the woman returned, all that was left of the camp was the charred bodies of the children. The woman was overcome with guilt and blamed herself for all of the dead children. In fact, she was so distraught by the horrible death the children suffered that she took her own life.

When I first heard this tragic tale about the death of so many young orphans, I had hoped that it would turn out to be nothing more than an urban legend. What I discovered about this nearly forgotten camp was not what I expected. It is an understatement that the real history of Camp Lady of the Lake is hard to find. Nearly everyone I spoke with was familiar with the haunted legends, yet no one had any specific information on the history of the camp. Skeptics claim that the whole legend was created by writer Linda M. Fields, who wrote a fictional story titled "Our Lady of the Lake." In my correspondence with Ms. Fields, she told me that although her story is indeed fiction, it was inspired by the real camp history. During my research of this case I was able to find that there was a Catholic camp called Camp Lady of the Lake that opened in 1954. According to the May 27, 1954 edition of *Mansfield News Journal*, the Michigan camp was open to both the boys and girls of the Toledo area. The camp was operated by the Toledo Catholic Charities Inc. and was a Catholic summer camp established by Msgr. Michael J. Doyle and run by the Sisters of the church.

A picturesque place for a camp

The camp was open to boys between the ages of 7 and 13 and girls from 7 to 15. The campers lived in small individual cabins and the activities were listed as water sports, arts, crafts, games, nature hikes, music, and campfires. The 1954 article does not specify that the children needed to be orphans in order to attend the camp. Contradicting this, however, is a July 8, 1970 article in the *Independent Newspaper* stating that the closed camp had indeed been used for Toledo area orphans. During my research I was unable to find the exact date of the camp's closing. I also uncovered a story from 1960 that stated the camp was hosting a meeting titled "Day of Recollection for Catholic girls in scouting." The 1970 article claimed that the camp had gone mostly unused for several years, which would put the closing of the camp sometime in the mid 1960s. During that time, a group of immigrant workers were camping out (squatting) in the area and were seeking permission to remain living there. It is believed that the original camp closed down due to constant flooding that ravaged the area. The church did not have the necessary funds to continually repair the structures, so they basically left the camp unused. I was unable to find any information that could prove or disprove the story of the camp leader committing suicide.

The seclusion of the area only adds to its creepiness

Regardless of how and when the camp shut down, one thing that remains certain is that those who visit often leave with a paranormal experience. Just like in Hollywood movies, it seems that much of the paranormal activity takes place late at night. The local dare states that if you visit the camp at night you will encounter the ghost of the woman whose guilt forced her to kill herself. Several local residents told me that they had heard the warning that you should not go out to the camp at night because of all the odd and mysterious things that will happen to you if you do. Researcher Linda Godfrey, on her website *Weird Michigan*, collected a story from a young girl who tagged along with some friends as they headed out to the camp at 2am. When the excited group first arrived at the old camp they began hearing some sort of sinister laughing coming from the woods which they bravely shrugged off, thinking it was only their imagination. A few moments later, the young woman saw the ghost of a little girl standing right in front of her. The ghostly little girl was wearing an old dress and was surrounded by an odd, glowing white light. Startled by the sudden appearance of the little girl, the group immediately took off running for the safety of their car. While she was in full sprint, the young woman felt that something had caught up to her and was pushing her from behind.

Little physical evidence of the camp still remains

When I finally stepped foot into the old camp grounds, I could immediately see why so many people believed the place was haunted. The place looked completely forgotten, surrounded by thick trees, unruly weeds, and overgrown vegetation—nature was doing its best to purge any painful memory of the camp's demise. Even with the gorgeous beach, it took a bit of imagination to visualize how beautiful the camp must have been. I am not alone in my creepy assessment of the location, as numerous legend trippers have gone to the camp late at night only to find themselves overwhelmed with an uneasy feeling that they were certainly not alone. After all my research into this case, I am still left with more questions than answers. Was the camp ravished by a deadly fire? Was the head woman so consumed with guilt that she took her own life? Until more history of the old camp surfaces, we may never know what truly took place deep in the dark woods. Locals take comfort in the belief that the ghost of the camp director keeps a protective watch over the spirits of the charred children who want to enjoy their time at camp, regardless of whether they are alive or dead.

The Killing of John Dillinger

Location:

Victory Gardens Biograph Theater—Formerly the Biograph Theater
2433 N. Lincoln Ave.
Chicago, IL 60614
(773) 871–3000
www.victorygardens.org

Haunting:

In 1934, the most wanted man in America was not some sick, demented serial killer or sadistic rapist, or even a disturbed child molester. No, America's

Public Enemy #1 was John Dillinger, bank robber extraordinaire. His rise and fall should serve as a cautionary tale against the ills of crime. Yet for a whole generation, Dillinger's suave personality and uncanny ability to elude capture capsulated America's new found distrust of government. As a bank robber, he was considered by many to be a folk hero. Secretly, and not so secretly, Americans envied his ability to the thwart the law, buck society's expectations and enjoy the freedom of the open road. Ironically, whenever Dillinger's wanted poster was shown on the screen before movies, audiences would actually stand up and applaud for him. It didn't hurt his cause that many of the largest banks had mismanaged their funds and were foreclosing on the homes and farms of millions of Americans. The general public didn't care that Dillinger was robbing banks, because they felt that the banks were robbing the general public.

You can partially blame Dillinger's infamy on the newspapers which printed daily accounts of his daring exploits. Yet even his immense fame and popularity could not stop his uncanny luck from eventually running out. After several years of fabulous escapes and amazing robberies, Dillinger was finally brought down by the betrayal of a woman. On July 22, 1934, John Dillinger was spending a night out on the town while enjoying a showing of the movie *Manhattan Melodrama*. Dillinger had no idea that he was being set up for capture. Anna Sage, a Romanian immigrant, was being threatened with deportation due to several illegal business dealings she was involved with. Having no interest in leaving the U.S., Sage believed that if she were to give the Feds the most wanted man in America, they would in turn let her stay in the country (they didn't). True to her word, when the movie finished Dillinger came strolling out of the Biograph Theater. According to the FBI, as soon as Dillinger exited the theater, he spotted the agents. He bolted toward the alley, where the Feds blasted him as he reached for his gun. Eyewitnesses of the shooting tell a much different story. Many claimed to see several law enforcement agents walk up behind an unknown man (Dillinger) and shoot him in the back without warning. No matter what version is true, if either, Dillinger bled to death in the alley waiting for help to arrive. Immediately, word starting spreading that the FBI had finally gotten Dillinger, and hundreds of people began gathering around the alleyway in order to catch a glimpse of the fallen gangster lying in a pool of his own blood. Dozens of curious onlookers were actually able to dip their newspaper or handkerchiefs into the blood to take home as a grisly souvenir.

Crowds gather around the blood of Dillinger

What makes this case so fascinating is that people have experienced paranormal activity in both the historic theater and in the alleyway where Dillinger took his last breath. Inside the historic theater many staff and visitors have had experiences that they simply cannot explain. The most common phenomenon is that of an apparition of a man dressed like he is from the early 1900s; he is spotted moving throughout the building. Although the witnesses only catch a glimpse of the passing spirit, they are convinced that it is the restless ghost of John Dillinger. It is said that the spirit of Dillinger is often spotted sitting in the very same seat that he watched his last movie from. Other patrons have been inside enjoying the entertainment when, out of nowhere, they are suddenly overcome with a bone freezing chill. The source of this mysterious roaming cold spot has never been discovered. When I visited the theater, it was under new management and the staff members I spoke with told me that, although they had heard of the theater's haunted reputation, they did not have any additional information to add. I got the sense that the new company was looking to distance itself from the theater's deadly past. While Terry Fisk and I were working on our first book, *The Wisconsin Road Guide to Haunted Locations*, we often encountered businesses that would insist that we didn't include them in our guide because they feared that if people found out their restaurant, hotel, B&B, etc. was haunted, it would negatively affect business. Eventually many of them relented, claiming that "no one is going to read that book anyway," and today we are flooded with email from places that now thank us for including them in our books due to the amount of business it generates. My hope is that the Biograph will one day come around and see the benefits of embracing their history, no matter how bloody it is.

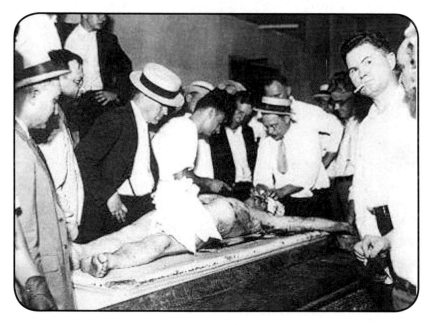

The bloody corpse of John Dillinger

If you are looking to have a paranormal encounter, you can skip the theater and hang out in the alleyway where Dillinger met his death. In her book,

Ghost Stories of Illinois, author Jo-Anne Christensen writes that those looking down what is known as "Dillinger's Alleyway" sometimes spotted "a shadowy blue figure running, stumbling, and disappearing upon contact with the ground." Those who have seen the ghostly man are not alone, as over the decades many unsuspecting passersby have seen the same ghostly image of a well-dressed man running through the alleyway. The sighting is usually followed with the phantom sounds of blasting gun fire, although no cause for the shots has ever been located. Based on the descriptions of the peculiarly clothed man, it is thought that Dillinger's ghost is looking to making one last break for it.

Murder at the Mansion

Location:

3300 London Road
Duluth, MN 55804
(218) 726–8910
www.d.umn.edu/glen

Haunting:

Perhaps in an effort to erase the horrific memories from their collective consciousness, many communities often try to remove all evidence of infamous events. In Wisconsin they burned down Ed Gein's house and tore down the apartment complex where Jeffery Dahmer lived, and Illinois demolished the site of the Valentine's Day Massacre. But the people of Minnesota are a bit different, because of instead of getting rid of their gruesome sites, they actually turn them into tourist destinations. This is exactly what happened to the Historic Congdon Estate of Duluth, better known as the Glensheen Mansion. Here, at perhaps the most recognizable home in all of Minnesota, they have a murder mystery straight out of the board game Clue.

This tragic story began in 1977, when Elisabeth Congdon bequeathed her family mansion to the University of Minnesota amid fears that her remaining relatives could not maintain or afford the upkeep of the estate. The contract allowed Elisabeth to remain in her home for as long as she lived. Little did she know that death was waiting around the next corner. On the night of June 27, 1977, an intruder broke into the mansion and made his way up towards Elisabeth's bedroom. Reaching the staircase, the intruder unexpectedly encountered Velma Pietila, who was working as Elisabeth's night nurse. Being of slight build and older age, the nurse was quickly overpowered and sent crashing to the floor. The intruder then grabbed a 12-inch brass candlestick holder from the top of the stairs and used it to bash the life out of the nurse. Covered in blood, the intruder then stalked his way up to Elisabeth's bedroom, hoping that the noise he created disposing of the nurse had not awoken his next victim. Upon entering the room, the intruder saw 84-year-old Elisabeth Congdon sleeping peacefully in her bed. The intruder carefully grabbed one of the pink satin pillows, placed it over Elisabeth's face, and held it tightly until he was positive Elisabeth had breathed her last breath. Within a matter of minutes, two women were dead, and the murderer got to work scooping up jewelry and various valuables from the home. Investigators believed that Marjorie Congdon (Elisabeth's daughter) was the mastermind behind the plan that sent her husband (Roger Caldwell) into the home to kill Elisabeth while she slept in order to collect the sizable inheritance. They had hoped that if the plan had gone correctly, no one would have questioned that a senior woman in poor health died in her sleep. All bets were thrown off as soon as Roger unexpectedly encountered the night nurse. As she arrived for work, the morning nurse had the displeasure of discovering the two dead bodies. It didn't take long for investigators to hone in on Roger and Marjorie and arrest them for the murder of Elizabeth Congdon. In 1978, a jury found Rodger guilty of murder and the judge gave him two consecutive life sentences. Marjorie was also arrested and put on trial for the murder of her mother. Astonishingly, contrary to all the evidence, the jury found her not guilty. In an odd twist to the story, when the case was completed, the jury threw a party and actually invited Marjorie along to celebrate. In yet another bizarre twist to the case, after the acquittal of Marjorie, Roger was awarded a new trial and just days before the fiasco was set to begin, Roger struck a deal with prosecutors whereby he would plead guilty to two counts of second degree murder and they would let him go free, having already served five years in prison. Many investigators researching the case claim that perhaps Marjorie may have gotten away with murder. Investigative reporter Joe Kimball chronicled in his book, *Secrets of the Congdon Mansion*, several mysterious events that followed Marjorie including numerous unexplained fires and the mysterious death of her second husband.

MURDER VICTIMS--Velma Pietila, left, and Elizabeth Congdon were murdered Sunday night or early Monday in Congdons Duluth, Minn., mansion. Pietila, Congdon's night nurse was found on a staircase landing. Her death was attributed to a blow from a heavy candlestick. Congdon was found in bed, smothered apparently with her pillow. (AP LASER-PHOTO)

The victims of the horrific murders

The Glensheen Mansion officially opened as a museum in 1979. From the beginning, the combination of breathtaking Jacobean Revival architecture, interesting Duluth history, and amazingly designed interior rooms made the tours extremely popular with the general public. Those looking to hear macabre details of the murder were solely disappointed, because workers remained extremely tight lipped about the deadly history of the home. Tour guides refused to answer any questions about the history at what the press had called the "death house." In the early 1990s, I started getting questions about the museum from curious visitors who had experienced something odd during their tours of the mansion. The majority of the reports I received came from people who claimed that as soon as they entered Elisabeth's bedroom, they were overcome with the sensation of being suffocated and struggled to breathe. Strangely, as soon as they stepped foot out of Elisabeth's room, the suffocating feeling immediately stopped as though they had crossed some invisible line. The staircase where the night nurse was murdered also produced many odd sensations, the most frequent symptom being the sudden uneasiness of the stomach as guests walked the staircase. Several visitors who were unaware of the home's odd history told me that as soon as they hit the staircase, they felt as though they were going to throw-up, but as soon as they left the staircase the urge to vomit disappeared. It was only after having such an unexpected reaction to the staircase that visitors began questioning the tour guides for an explanation.

The Death House

I was fortunate enough to have the opportunity to tour the mansion and speak with several staff members who told me strange things often happen at Glensheen. One of the supervisors shared with me a bizarre encounter that happened to one of his former employees. The worker was positioned high up on a ladder while doing some maintenance on the roof when he felt the sensation of someone (or something) tugging at his ankle. Thinking that it would have been impossible for anyone to have climbed up the ladder without his knowing, the man quickly looked down at his foot just in time to see a human hand disappear into thin air. Freaked out, the man scrambled down the ladder, went home, and refused to return to work. His supervisor told me that he was a great employee but after his odd experience, he simply would not come back to the mansion. Many of the employees I interviewed reported that the majority of the paranormal incidents that they had experienced were not overly frightening. They cited little, odd things that at first glance did not seem to be outright paranormal in nature. Objects that were placed in one spot would often be found in a completely different spot, shadows would be seen moving down empty hallways, and unusual noises echoed through the building.

A few years ago I was in Duluth giving a lecture on the most haunted places in Minnesota, when a gentleman approached me and claimed that he knew for certain that the Glensheen Mansion was haunted. It turned out that the man was employed with the company that operates the mansion's security system. The worker was frustrated by the fact that every couple of nights the mansion's security system would be triggered, forcing him to go and make sure no one had broken into the place. Each and every time the man responded, he found the place completely empty. All of the doors and windows were secure, there were no signs of any intruders, no animals or rodents had found their way in, and by all accounts the visits always turned out to be false alarms. It was during these visits that the man became convinced that something out of the ordinary was taking place at Glensheen. Refusing to go into great detail, the man told me that on several occasions he had come face to face with a female spirit that he believed was one of the women who met their end at the mansion. With so much unsolved activity happening at the mansion, the staff may fare better by forgoing asking visiting children to count to the number of pineapple carvings inside and instead have them count up the number of wandering spirits.

A Ghostly Family Reunion

Location:

Crouch–Reynolds Cemetery—Corner of Reynolds Road and Horton Drive
Jacob Crouch's Grave—The unmarked grave is located just to the right of
the main gate under the spirea bush.
Jackson, MI

Haunting:

Every year, a father and his loving daughter reunite in a small rural cemetery
in the middle of nowhere. Neighbors report that this family rendezvous
has been occurring for quite some time. Their annual meeting is not too

inconvenient, as the father doesn't have far to travel and his daughter is located less than five miles away. The only thing that makes this case odd is the fact that both the father and daughter have been dead for over 100 years.

It is believed that the spirits haunting the cemetery are those of a father and daughter who were murdered in 1883. Here is the scenario that the investigators put together after the murders. Sometime during the late evening of November 21/ morning of November 22, someone entered the Crouch farm and brutally shot four people as they were sleeping.

The Crouch family farm

Victims:

Jacob Crouch—The seventy-four-year-old man was believed to be one of the wealthiest farmers in Michigan. Four years prior to his death, Jacob had purchased a 15,000-acre ranch in Texas that was said to be worth over $1 million. It was believed that Jacob had just received a huge sum of money generated from several ranches he operated in Texas. Jacob's body was discovered with a gunshot wound behind his left ear and one in the neck. According to the *Galveston Daily*, Jacob was the only victim that showed evidence of a struggle with his killers.

Jacob Crouch

Eunice White (Jacob's daughter)—Eunice was in the final stages of her pregnancy when the intruders blasted her with five shots, two in the right arm, one in her right wrist, one through her lungs, and one in her lower jaw.

Henry White (Eunice's husband)—Henry was shot twice. One shot struck an artery in the right side of his head, while the other shot entered his right temple near his eye.

Moses Polley (A visitor)—Moses was a Pennsylvania cattleman that had traveled to Michigan to conduct some business with Crouch. Mr. Polley was found with a hole in the back of his neck.

Those who survived:

Julie Reese (A domestic)—Julie claimed that she had slept through the whole affair, even though her quarters were only 25 feet away from where the shootings occurred.

George Boles (A young servant)—When questioned by investigators, George first claimed that he knew nothing of the deaths. George later changed his story, telling officials that after hearing what sounded like gunfire, he jumped into a nearby chest and hid there all night. However, investigators pointed out that chest that George claimed to have hidden in was much too small for him to have fit into. George was held by police but was eventually released.

Evidence:

Gun—Investigators found several empty cartridges on the floor indicating that during his/her killing spree the murderer had reloaded. All of the balls (bullets) were of the same size, leading to the conclusion that only one weapon was used in the murders.

Tracks Outside—Investigators found a pair of tracks outside in the snow leading them to believe that someone may have stood guard in the yards while the murders were taking place inside the home.

Chloroform—The *Janesville Daily Gazette* reported that the once word of the killings got out, curious neighbors who rushed to the house smelled a strong scent of chloroform in the air, raising the theory that some of the victims may have been drugged before they were killed. This contrasted the report from several doctors that claimed no chloroform was used.

Theories explaining the murders:

Jud Crouch (Jacob's son) and **Dan Holcomb** (Jacob's son-in-law) were arrested and held for the murders because it was thought that the two men had committed the crime for their father's money. Both men were charged with the murders, but both were found innocent by a jury.

Railroad Passengers—One of the most credible theories of the murders is that on his way to Michigan, Mr. Polley bragged about his wealth and perhaps even flashed a lot of money around the train. This type of behavior attracted some of the less-desirable characters who then followed him to Jacob's home, and the robbery turned into murder.

Paranormal activity:

Surprisingly, the haunted activity does not happen at the old farm where the murders took place. Instead, the strange happenings take place in the cemetery where Jacob Crouch was laid to rest. Shortly after the horrific murders took place, nearby neighbors began reporting that a mysterious floating mist would often hover around the cemetery before disappearing over Crouch's gravesite. It is not known if there was ever a stone marking his grave. If there was, it was long ago stolen or lost, as Crouch currently rests in an unmarked grave.

A paranormal meeting place

The main version of this legend is that each year, on the anniversary of the murders, the spirit of Eunice White rises up from her grave in the nearby St. John Catholic Cemetery and travels to Crouch-Reynolds Cemetery to once again be reunited with her lost father. The ghostly white mist that has been appearing over the grave of Jacob is believed to be the disembodied spirit of Eunice trying to be close to her father. Whether the mist is that of Crouch or his daughter, it always seems to dissipate when it reaches his grave. Others contend that it is actually Crouch, the loving father, who rises up and makes his way down to Eunice's gravesite.

It was summertime when I investigated this case, and even though many locals had stories of seeing the mist throughout the year, legend states that those fortunate enough to be in the area on November 21 will be treated to the sight of Eunice and Jacob's spirits reuniting from the grave. My advice to those looking to make the trip to this secluded cemetery—mark your calendars for November 21.

The Demented Cannibal
Milwaukee, Wisconsin

The Demented Cannibal

Location:

Ambassador Hotel
2308 West Wisconsin Avenue
Milwaukee, WI 53233
(414) 342–8400
www.ambassadormilwaukee.com

Haunting:

If you were to check in to the swanky Ambassador Hotel today, you would never in a million years guess that the hotel could have once served as a grungy hookup spot for two young men looking to have a cheap night of passion together. Even harder to imagine is that the night of wild sex would bring forth a morning of murder and cover-up. This case began back in 1987, when Milwaukee resident Jeffery Dahmer made a habit of frequenting local gay bars so he could proposition men with promises of money, booze, and graphic adult movies. In his 160-page confession, Dahmer claimed that he often went out to the bars with the forgone conclusion that he was going to kill someone. While staying at the lowly downtown Ambassador Hotel, he stalked out potential victims. Dahmer's plan was to lure young men back to his place, spike their drinks with Halcion tablets, have sex with them while they were unconscious, and then kill them before they could leave. Sometime around Easter of 1987, he put his sick plan into action when he persuaded Michael Salinas and C'est La Vie to accompany him back to his place for some drinks. Salinas told the *Milwaukee Journal* that "after arriving at the hotel room, Dahmer took off all his clothes and invited him

Arrest photo of Dahmer

and his friend to do the same but they declined." Dahmer then poured each of them a rum drink and the next thing Salinas recalled was waking up on the floor of the room with his pants unbuckled and his friend passed out on the bed. Dahmer was nowhere to be found, so the two foggy headed men quickly left the hotel. A few years later, Salinas and La Vie would find out just how lucky they were.

After making a few practice runs of drugging and raping his victims, Dahmer was now ready to add murder to his list. Stalking out the gay clubs, he invited 24-year-old Steve Tuomi back to his rented room at the Ambassador Hotel for a few drinks. After a few spiked rums, Dahmer performed several sexual acts with the passed out man before calling it a night. According to the *Daily Globe*, Dahmer apparently gave Tuomi "a heavier dose of the drug than he intended." The next morning Dahmer woke up and discovered that Tuomi was dead, even though he couldn't remember what happened. Dahmer calmly added another day on to his room rental and left Tuomi's body there as he went out to buy the largest suitcase his could find. Upon his return, Dahmer stuffed the dead man into his newly bought suitcase and left the hotel. A taxi cab dropped Dahmer and his dead companion off at his grandmother's house where he began smashing some of the bones with a sledgehammer. The rest of the body was chopped up into chunks and disposed of it in the garbage. The sexual gratification Dahmer received from handling Tuomi's dead body only intensified his demented urge to strike again. When all was said and done, Dahmer admitted to killing 17 young men in a bizarre attempt to make sexual zombies that he could force into doing whatever he wanted them to do. The *Wisconsin State Journal* reported on many of the more gruesome details of this case, writing that Dahmer would "cut the flesh into fist-sized chunks and pack them into bags, which he disposed of in the trash," and that "the average body took up five 25-gallon garbage bags (each one triple

lined to prevent leakage." The paper added, "Dahmer related that the skin of the human being was easily detached... much the way you would detach skin from a chicken." He also told police that he had eaten several body parts from three of his victims, including one heart, a bicep, and thigh muscle.

Unknown figures have been seen moving down hallways

What investigators found in Dahmer's apartment could have served as a set of a horror movie. A human head was chilling in the fridge, other severed heads decorated his bedroom, and several detached penises were lying around, along with scores of pictures showing different bodies in various stages of decomposition. In 1992, Dahmer was found guilty on 15 counts of murder and sentenced to 15 life sentences at the Columbia Correctional Institution in Portage, Wisconsin. However, he would only serve two years of his sentence before he was beaten to death by another inmate.

Many believe the spirit of Dahmer's victim haunts the hotel

The terrible memory of Dahmer still haunts many locations throughout Milwaukee where he preyed on victims in order to quench his sadist sexual appetite. One place that would rather not keep alive this gruesome history is the newly renovated Ambassador Hotel. Plagued with being the place where Dahmer committed his first Milwaukee murder (and maybe others). When I spoke with the hotel's management they informed me that they normally refrain from talking about Dahmer, partly because of the gruesome nature, but mostly because they simply do not know anything outside of what the media released from court records. The upscale hotel understandably looks to forget its ghastly past. The only problem is that several spirits are hell bent on keeping that past alive. On several nights, hotel guests have reported seeing the ghostly image of a bloody man roaming the hotel—only to disappear into thin air. Odd banging and rapping noises can be heard throughout the hotel, seemingly coming out of nowhere. Guests have also reported hearing the loud voices of two men engaged in a heated argument or fight, but the source of this mystery brawl can never be located. It is believed that all of the paranormal activity is linked to Jeffery Dahmer and the victim that never escaped from his deadly web of sadistic seduction

Spirit Lake Massacre

Arnolds Park, Iowa

Spirit Lake Massacre

Location:

Abbie Gardner Cabin
Monument Drive
Arnolds Park, Iowa
(712) 332–7248
Open Memorial Day through September
Free Admission (donations appreciated)
www.iowahistory.org

Haunting:

In today's world of endless modern conveniences we tend to forget how taxing and troublesome life was for the pioneers. Droughts, fires, infectious diseases, and starvation were just a few of the tribulations that faced our ancestors. We also have conveniently swept away the great battles that were fought between the newly formed pioneer outposts and the Native American settlements that were already there. One place that has not forgotten the past is the Abbie Gardner Historic Site which strives to keep alive the memory of the gruesome 1857 Spirit Lake Massacre that soiled the land with blood.

In the summer of 1856, Rowland (Rolland) Gardner and his family made the strenuously dangerous trek from New York to Iowa on ox drawn wagons bursting with all their worldly possessions. Settling in the area, Gardner built a small log cabin on the shore of Lake Okoboji. The Gardners knew that many Indians still resided in the area, but considered them friendly—a mistake that would soon become deadly. In 1857, a band of Sioux Indians migrated to the area lead by Chief Inkpaduta, who, it is safe to say, was no fan of the white man. One evening while eating dinner, the Gardners heard the distinct sounds of a Native American war dance. Having never experienced any trouble from the Indians in the past, the Gardners made the fateful error of ignoring these warning signs. The very next morning while they were enjoying a quiet breakfast, they received an uninvited guest. The "guest" was a tall unknown Indian who walked right into the cabin without as much as a knock. Startled by the uninvited visitor, Mrs. Gardner offered the man a plate of food, which he graciously accepted. Moments later, 14 more Indians gathered at the cabin also looking for food. Becoming a bit more fearful, Mrs. Gardner happily gave them what little food she had on hand. After their meals, the Indians exited the cabin but suspiciously stuck around the area. By now the Gardners were fully worried and sent two young men off to warn the rest of the villagers. The Gardners had no idea that the young men had been shot dead by the Indians before any warning could be given. Just as darkness set in, the Indians came back and demand all of the Gardner's supplies. As Mr. Gardner turned to gather up what he could, the Indians killed him with a shot through the back. They then set about killing all of the Gardner family sparing only Abbie, the youngest of the Gardner children, who was taken as an Indian prisoner.

Psychics regularly sense many spirits at Abbie's cabin

For the next few weeks, Abbie was forced to watch as she traveled with the Indians as they killed several other villagers, taking even more prisoners. A visitor happened to stumble upon the brutal murders and ran off of to warn other nearby settlers. This time the messenger arrived safely at Fort Dodge and was able to alert the authorities. At the time, there were not enough men at the fort to realistically fight off the Indians so they decided to send out a couple of men to give the dead settlers a proper burial. It was an especially brutal winter that took the lives of several of the men who joined the dead settlers that they were supposed to be burying. Three months later, the Indians decided to give Abbie Gardner back to the village in exchange for some horses, blankets, tobacco, and gun powder. With this human exchange, Abbie was once again free. Soon after her release, she married Cassville Sharp and they had two children.

Monument put up for those who lost their lives in the massacre

Years later, Abbie left her husband, moved back to her father's cabin in Arnolds Park and decided to open it up to the public as Iowa's first tourist attraction. Abbie would both delight and frighten curious visitors with the tantalizing stories of her capture and of the days she spent with the Indians. Despite all the tragedy, Abbie dearly loved her home… so it may come as no surprise that many people feel her spirit continues to haunt it to this very day. Those who visit the old cabin report feeling as though they were surrounded by spirits. For some visitors, an even more bizarre experience takes place when they return to their home. The historic site has received several calls from past visitors who believed that a spirit from the site had followed them home from the cabin. One disgruntled caller claimed that a spirit from the cabin had somehow attached itself to her and was now responsible for rearranging her furniture whenever she goes out.

Does the spirit of Abbie still wander the grounds?

Psychics often visit the site in hopes that they might make contact with any of the spirits haunting the area. Many of them have been overwhelmed with the feelings of death and sadness pouring out from those who met their fate at the site. Not all psychics pick up on the negative, as many other psychics report sensing the kind and friendly spirit of Abbie Gardner who is continuing to keep a watchful eye over her place. Don't worry—you don't have to be a psychic to feel a presence at the site. I spoke with the site's director who informed me that many regular visitors to the area feel that the spirits of those who died in the massacre are still there and can be felt by those willing to open themselves up to it.

Author Bio

Chad Lewis—Is a researcher, author, and lecturer on topics of the strange and unusual. Since 1992, Chad has traveled the back roads of the world in search of the strange and unusual. From tracking vampires in Transylvania and searching for the elusive monster of Loch Ness to trailing the dangerous Tata Duende through remote villages of Belize and searching for ghosts in Ireland's haunted castles, Chad has scoured the earth in search of the paranormal. With a Masters Degree in Psychology, Chad has authored over 15 books on the supernatural, and extensively lectures on his fascinating findings. The more bizarre the legend, the more likely you'll find Chad there.

To reach Chad, go to his websites:

www.unexplainedresearch.com or www.chadlewisresearch.com

You can also email him at chadlewis44@hotmail.com

Other Titles Authored/Co-Authored by Chad Lewis

Haunted Places

The Illinois Road Guide to Haunted Locations

The Iowa Road Guide to Haunted Locations

The Florida Road Guide to Haunted Locations

The Minnesota Road Guide to Haunted Locations

The South Dakota Road Guide to Haunted Locations

The Wisconsin Road Guide to Haunted Locations

Haunted St. Paul

General Paranormal

Hidden Headlines of New York

Hidden Headlines of Texas

Hidden Headlines of Wisconsin

The Wisconsin Road Guide to Mysterious Creatures

The Minnesota Road Guide to Mysterious Creatures

Gangsters

The Minnesota Road Guide to Gangster Hot Spots

The Wisconsin Road Guide to Gangster Hot Spots